# Team-Based Project Management

# TEAM-BASED PROJECT MANAGEMENT

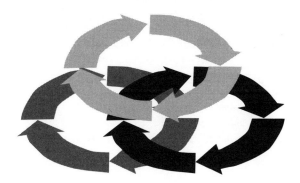

## JAMES P. LEWIS

### AMACOM
American Management Association

New York • Atlanta • Boston • Chicago • Kansas City • San Francisco • Washington, D.C.
Brussels • Mexico City • Tokyo • Toronto

This book is available at a special
discount when ordered in bulk quantities.
For information, contact Special Sales Department,
AMACOM, a division of American Management Association,
1601 Broadway, New York, NY 10019.

This publication is designed to provide accurate and authoritative information in regard to the subject matter covered. It is sold with the understanding that the publisher is not engaged in rendering legal, accounting, or other professional service. If legal advice or other expert assistance is required, the services of a competent professional person should be sought.

Library of Congress Cataloging-in-Publication Data

Lewis, James P., 1941–
    Team-based project management / James P. Lewis.
       p.  cm.
    Includes bibliographical references and index.
    ISBN 0-8144-0364-6 (hardcover)
    1. Project management.   2. Teams in the workplace.   I. Title.
HD69.P75L494   1997
658.4'04 — dc21                                  97-26629
                                                     CIP

Printing number

10   9   8   7   6   5   4   3

*This book is dedicated to*
*Dr. David Antonioni*
*a respected colleague and good friend.*

# Contents

# Preface

In her frustration with the men in her life, cartoon Kathy (Kathy Guise-white) says, "Men should come with instruction manuals!" I have known more than one project manager who felt the same as Kathy. Cars, equipment, VCRs, and machines come with instruction manuals that tell you how to get the most out of your investment. Yet human resources come with no such instructions, and much of their effort is wasted or poorly utilized. In today's downsized organizations, you can't afford to waste *any* of your human "capital." This book is written to help both new and experienced project managers overcome that problem.

Literally millions of project scheduling software programs have been sold in the United States alone. But, as many of the users of those programs have found, the tools do not make of you a project manager. Interest in project management is at an all-time high as shown by the growth in membership of the Project Management Institute, enrollment in seminars, and attendance at project management conferences. Yet a study by the Standish Group found that of the $250 billion spent in the United States on software development projects in 1994, only 17 percent of these projects met their original targets, while 50 percent had their targets significantly revised, and the remaining 33 percent were canceled. Although the money may not have been distributed linearly, this suggests that as much as $80 billion in project costs was flushed down the toilet! Clearly, something needs to be done.

One reason for the problem is that most attention is given to the *tools* of project management—Work Breakdown Structures, PERT/CPM or Gantt schedules, and perhaps earned value analysis—and very little regard is given to the human element. Yet most of the work that goes into projects is done by people, and too many project managers do not have the required skills in dealing with people to get the job done.

There is a tacit assumption in this country, expressed by our actions, that anyone who can do the technical aspects of a job can be a manager.

The assumption is expressed by the fact that we make managers of individuals without giving them any formal training in managing, and then wonder why they are not as effective as we think they should be. This is akin to giving someone a high-performance race car without any training in driving it. In fact, I have often thought that a person should have a "people-operating license" before being allowed to manage.

Over and over again managers who attend my seminar, Project Management: Tools, Principles, Practices, ask, "How do you get someone to . . . ?" Or "How do you handle the situation when . . . ?" This book is a response to all those people who have agonized over such questions. However, a word of caution is in order: In the same way that a race car driver has to learn the *principles* of racing in order to succeed, so too must you learn the *principles* of dealing with people. There are no formulas that say, "If you take steps 1, 2, and 3, you are guaranteed success." I wish there were, but there aren't.

As an example, I don't believe you can teach a person to be a good car mechanic by saying, "Now when you hear the engine make this kind of noise, turn this screw 90 degrees counterclockwise." If the mechanic does not understand the principles behind how an engine works, I don't think he will be very good.

The same is true for people and teams. No one can tell you, "If a person on your team stands on his head and crows like a chicken, here is what you should do." The best we can do is offer principles that explain how people and teams function and give you some examples of how these are applied. One of these that I find helpful is *people don't argue with their own data*. This principle helps me understand that if I want people to accept some information, I must help them discover it for themselves. If I preach to them or pontificate, they may reject my data. If they find it themselves, they accept it.

Such principles, if used properly, will help you solve many of your people problems and will enable you to bring in your projects on time, within budget, and without having a nervous breakdown! Happy sailing!

J.P.L.

# Acknowledgments

This book would not exist were it not for the encouragement of my acquisitions editor at AMACOM, Tony Vlamis. My previous teambuilding book, *How to Build and Manage a Winning Project Team,* is now out of print, and Tony wanted to do an entirely different kind of book, but with a team focus. I greatly appreciate his vote of confidence and his support over the years.

This is the second book project I have worked on with associate editor Barbara Horowitz. She has always been very helpful in making the final editing process as painless as it can be for someone like me (I hate for anyone to mess with my writing).

Most of the academic knowledge that I have about teams I got from the classes I took with Dr. Jim Luginbuhl, at North Carolina State University. Those were some of the most enjoyable college classes I ever took. Fortunately, I was able to extend the classroom work to my job, where my teammates were "guinea pigs." To them I owe a debt of thanks for putting up with my experimentation.

Since I became a consultant in 1981, I have worked with thousands of people who have attended my seminars, or who have been members of my client companies. Any instructor or consultant who doesn't learn as much from his clients and students as he teaches them probably isn't paying attention. Just the questions and challenges alone are invaluable, since they force you to think about and clarify your understanding of your subject. Thanks to all of you who have been part of that process.

As usual, my wife, Lea Ann, has made this book more interesting than it would have been if it were my effort alone. She has a great knack for finding just the right way to enhance the text with artwork that speaks to the reader. Many people who read my published books or class workbooks compliment me on how nice they look. The credit for how they look goes entirely to her.

Another person who has contributed greatly to my understanding of human beings is Dr. Paul Watzlawick. I have never met him, but his books have been the most enjoyable and insightful I have ever read. I very much appreciate his contribution to all of us who are trying to understand that enigmatic creature that Dr. Elliot Aronson has called "the Social Animal."

Finally, I want to thank Dr. David Antonioni, who is the director of the Project Management Certificate Series at the University of Wisconsin, Madison, for his continued support and friendship. I started working with David in 1991, teaching "Project Planning, Scheduling, and Control," and since that time we have had many fruitful conversations on all aspects of psychology, project management, and project teams. We have cofacilitated a number of seminars on teams, as well as several Future Search Conferences, and those have been exceptionally rewarding experiences for me. It is in appreciation of our friendship that I have dedicated this book to David.

As these acknowledgments always say, the credit for the strengths of the book go to all of these people. The weaknesses are entirely attributable to me. I hope they are inconsequential.

# SECTION ONE

# Project Management Concepts

# CHAPTER 1

# Introduction to Team-Based Project Management

Several years ago I was in Las Cruces, New Mexico, to teach a project management seminar for a group at NASA's White Sands Test Facility. The fellow who brought me into the organization gave me a tour of the town, which included a visit to the jail that was once a temporary home to Billy the Kid. The next day, on my way to the Space Center, I was struck by how desolate this country must have been in the days of Billy the Kid. As I drove through miles of scrub brush and rocky hills, I remembered a scene from an old Western movie (the name of which I have forgotten) in which one of the cowboys told how important it was to take good care of your horse, because your life depended on that horse. No cowboy in his right mind would abuse his horse, or he might wind up dead in that hostile country.

I have often thought that we could learn a lot from that cowboy because, unless you are working on one-person projects, your organizational life as a project manager depends on the performance of the people who make up your team. Yet most of our attention seems to be directed at the *tools* of project management. In fact, we could easily name most approaches to project management *Schedule-Based Project Management* because that tends to be our primary focus.

However, we know that the actual work gets done by *people*, and that we must therefore find ways to get the best possible performance from them. Indeed, it is often because of "people problems" that we have difficulty in applying the tools themselves.

The most common question asked in my seminars given to more than 1,000 project managers each year is, "How do you get someone to do [something—often something totally distasteful]? There are others: How do you get people to be committed to the project? How do you motivate

3

them? How do you get them to take deadlines seriously? How do you keep them from killing each other? And the list goes on and on.

Continuing with my thoughts on cowboys and their horses, I feel certain that riders in the "untamed West" were taught a few principles of horsemanship. Maybe not to the extent of a professional rider, but certainly enough to know how to ride a horse without killing it, and they learned how to conserve its strength and endurance when riding long distances. Managers, on the other hand, often arrive at their positions with no training in "humanship" and (figuratively) ride their horses to death. Unfortunately, as Kathy Guisewhite lamented (in her cartoon strip *Kathy*), "Men [don't] come with instruction manuals."

So I have written one.

This book is your guide on how to get the best from people in your project team, whether you are organized so that they all report to you 100 percent of the time or whether they are assigned to your project only on a part-time basis. It is not, however, a book on how to take advantage of people. It is not on how to manipulate them or on how to bleed them dry and then throw them onto a garbage heap.

In fact, I believe that much of the difficulty we managers encounter is because many Americans are stressed out, tuned out, and turned off, in part because they believe their organizations see them only as a necessary evil. As Michael Lerner (1996) has written about the findings of a study he conducted, ". . . we were surprised to discover that . . . middle Americans often experience more stress from feeling that they are wasting their lives doing meaningless work than from feeling that they are not making enough money."

No doubt a horse must be properly fed, watered, and rested in order to perform at its optimum. So, too, human beings must be properly cared for. You can't get something for nothing. However, unlike a horse, people need more than a paycheck (the equivalent of feed, water, and rest) in order to be fulfilled. People want to feel that their work is *meaningful*, that it counts for something. Yet many of them never know how their individual job fits into the whole. This is true of assembly line workers for certain, but it is also true of knowledge workers. I know programmers who design screens, develop databases, and so on without ever seeing the software applied in a real-world environment. The same is true of engineers. They design a component of a product without ever seeing that product used in its final application.

It is my conviction that this alone accounts for a major portion of the performance problems we have in teams, and I also firmly believe that we can solve this problem. I believe that a major responsibility of a project manager is to help members of the team find meaning in the work they do on that project, to help them feel that they are contributing, that their work is valued, and that they have been responsible for a successful outcome. If we can do that, many of our problems of motivation and commitment will be solved. If we do not achieve this result, then we will continue to suffer from apathy, back stabbing, and all the other ills that often afflict projects.

If you are willing to work with people in a win-win, mutually beneficial way, this book will tell you how to be successful. (If you aren't, no book will do you much good.) It is based on everything I have learned during the past thirty years as a working project manager, as a doctoral student of psychology, and as a consultant to organizations. It may not contain answers to every problem you will ever encounter, but it does contain *principles* that will guide you in solving every problem you will ever have. That is the best we can ever do.

I recently received a call from a fellow who attended one of my project management classes. He told me that he had just been on a flight and was reading *How to Build and Manage a Winning Project Team*, a book I wrote for AMACOM several years ago. He had also been reading the Bible. He went to the lavatory and left both books on the seat. When he came back, he found that someone had stolen the team book but had left the Bible. We both had a good laugh. If this thief thinks my book is going to help him succeed with his teams, he is sadly mistaken. No set of *techniques* will overcome a lack of character.

However, you *do* need methods, principles, and tools. I was originally trained as an electrical engineer. We learned Ohm's Law, Maxwell's laws, semiconductor theory, and so on, so that we could apply those principles in our work to solve technical problems. Likewise, if you learn the principles of dealing with people, you can apply them to any problem you may have with members of your team.

What is important to note is that the principles themselves must be valid. It seems reasonable to say that if a guiding principle is wrong, you can hardly expect to achieve a desired outcome by applying it. As Meg Wheatley (1994) and many other writers have shown in recent years, much of our thinking has been influenced by seventeenth-century science. That science was based on Newton's conception of the universe as a big clockwork mechanism, in which energy stored in a "spring" ran the whole thing. In order to understand the whole, we had only to break the clock down into its parts. This reductionist approach has served us well in some respects, and has done us a great disservice in others.

In understanding organizations, for example, it has led to the belief that we can look at the individual parts to comprehend the whole. As a natural extension of that belief, we have all been taught that if we improve one part of the organization, we will automatically improve the overall "thing." This is simply not true in many cases. Dr. W. Edwards Deming, Russell Ackoff, and recently Peter Senge have cautioned against such sub-optimization. We have all seen examples in which one department was optimized, with dire consequences for other groups. To illustrate why this is so, Russell Ackoff likes to say that if we were to go around the world collecting the best components of all the world's cars, then assembled them to make a new car, we probably wouldn't have a very good car. The reason: The parts have not been *jointly optimized*, which is necessary to make the whole entity perform well.

We also learn from New Science that the world is not entirely like the world described by Newtonian physics. Fractal geometry, chaos theory, self-organizing systems, and particle physics have shed new light on the world that demands that we rethink our organizations and—consequently—our management methods.

One component of Newtonian physics that has greatly influenced our thinking about organizations and psychology was the importance given to *energy*. In organizations, we believed that a command-and-control approach was necessary in order to achieve *control*. Left to themselves, human beings would wander around chaotically wasting time and money. Only if a manager adopted a hard-nosed, butt-kicking approach could he overcome the *inertia* (note the energy connotation) inherent in people and get them off their behinds so they would do useful work. Naturally they could be expected to *resist* (another energy word), so a manager had to know how to *motivate* (ditto) them. We talk about building our *power* bases as managers, how to gain *clout*, and how to build a *winning team!* (All of these refer to energy, and even my first book on team building was entitled *How to Build and Manage a Winning Project Team*.)

In psychology, Freud believed that trauma caused energy to be stored in the human psyche and that some catharsis was required to release it and thus free the person from the limitations imposed by the trauma. (He never explicitly said where that energy was stored, but his emphasis on sex suggests that he thought the energy was stored in the reproductive organs.)

Unfortunately, Freudian theory and methodology have (in my opinion) been dismally ineffective in freeing people from their neuroses, psychoses, and other psychological problems, and I believe it is because the model was incorrect in the first place. (For a good exposition of why this is so, see Jay Haley's *Strategies of Psychotherapy*, 1986). Much the same can be said for the practices of management. Practices based on power and energy have not been very effective, so it is time to look for a more useful paradigm, or model of what the world is like.

New Science has taught us that we can understand systems much better through an *information model*, rather than one based on energy. Thus, the definition of control that should be applied to organizations (and especially to project management) is: *Control is exercised by comparing where we are to where we are supposed to be, so that corrective action can be taken to get us back on track when there is a deviation.* This is entirely based on information, not power, and casts a very different light on how management should be exercised.

In this book, I have drawn on this and other principles from New Science to suggest ways in which we should manage projects differently than we have done in the past. Because New Science challenges many of our old paradigms, some of these ideas at first seem strange, perhaps even wrong, but that always happens when new paradigms are displacing the old. (See Barker, 1992, for a fuller treatment of paradigms.) All any of us can do is keep an open mind, experiment, and find out if the new models yield better results than the old.

One of physicist Werner Heisenberg's legacies was his Uncertainty Principle, which suggests that we can never be *absolutely* certain that our models are correct. At best, we can only say that they are *useful*. So, I make no assertion that my principles are absolutely correct. I simply say that I have found them to be useful, and hope that you will too.

With that understanding, let's move on to how you can succeed with team-based project management!

# CHAPTER 2

# A Brief Review of Some Project Management Concepts

Although I am writing this book for the reader who already knows the tools of project management, I know that not everyone uses the same terms or approaches to managing projects. For that reason, it might be helpful to briefly summarize some essential concepts of project management so that you will be familiar with my ideas. If you feel very confident that this is old hat to you, feel free to skip this chapter.

The first order of business is to define what we mean by a project. I define a project as a job that is done one time. It should have a definite starting point, a definite ending point, and usually a schedule and budget for how the work will be done. If an activity is repetitive, such as manufacturing or processing insurance claims, it is not a

> A project is a job that is done one time.

project. Certainly these conditions are ideal. In practice, many projects seem to go on forever, have no clear schedule or budget, and sometimes not even a clear starting point. However, this ideal should be the target toward which we aim our efforts.

The second concept that is important to define is what we mean by project management. We say that it is the planning, scheduling, and controlling of scarce resources to achieve desired results. These results are defined in terms of four factors, called Cost, Schedule, Performance, and Scope. Cost and schedule are well known. Scope is the magnitude of the job. Performance has to do with how well team members do their work. The level of their performance will, of course, affect the performance of the product or service they produce. As a fellow told me recently, you can

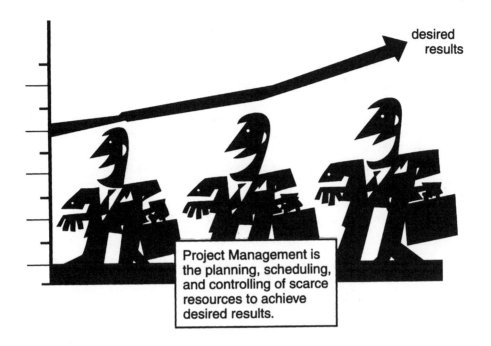

desired results

Project Management is the planning, scheduling, and controlling of scarce resources to achieve desired results.

be over budget, behind schedule, and a little under scope so long as the "thing" works when you finish, and people will forgive you. But if you are late, over budget, under scope, and it still doesn't work, you're in big trouble! He's right.

The relationship of these performance criteria to each other is given by the equation:

$$C = f(P, T, S)$$

The equation reads, "Cost is a function of Performance, Time, and Scope." Performance is the quality of work done by the project team and Scope is the magnitude of the work they must do. As mentioned previously, Cost will be the money spent on the project, or the project budget, and Time will be the duration of the project.

**Principle:** You can assign values to any three of the four variables, but the fourth will be whatever the "equation" says it will be.

It is especially important to note that you can assign values to any three of these variables, but the fourth one will be whatever the equation dictates. For example, it is customary for project managers to be told the deadline for the project (Time), the level of quality expected(Performance), and the magnitude of the work (Scope). The project manager then should figure out what resources are needed to achieve these targets, which will determine the Cost of the program.

Unfortunately, senior managers sometimes tell the project manager that the job must also be completed for a certain cost, meaning that they have assigned values to all four variables in the equation. In many cases the numbers don't work, and the project is doomed to failure from the beginning.

Because you will always be making tradeoffs among these four performance measures, you should know the relationship equation cold.

# Project Management Versus General Management

What is the difference between managing in general and managing projects? Naturally, there are commonalities, but I believe the major differences are in the one-time nature of projects, their strong attention to schedule, and the fact that most general managers have a full-time team that reports to them, whereas project managers often have teams assigned only for the duration of the project. Further, in the case of a matrix organization (see Figure 2-1), the members of the team still report to functional managers.

This kind of organization creates tremendous problems for the project manager that the general manager does not have. People assigned to the project team may have no loyalty or commitment to the team; they may see the project manager as a nuisance; and they may therefore be very uncooperative. Many project managers lament that they have a lot of responsibility but absolutely no authority! And this is true.

Another difference between managing projects and general management is that project managers are often dealing with work for which it is very difficult to estimate durations, costs, and resource requirements, because the work is new or it has been done only a few times. Yet everyone wants to know before the project starts how long will it take and how much will it cost. Answering these questions may require a crystal ball.

The general manager, on the other hand, is often dealing with repetitive tasks that have enough history for times and costs to be known. (Note that this is only true of lower-level managers. Because senior executives are frequently dealing with new situations they share some of the difficul-

**Figure 2-1.** Example of a matrix organization.

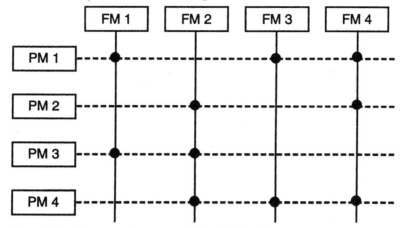

Note: FM = Functional Manager; PM = Project Manager.

ties that face project managers.) So if the general manager is asked to produce so many goodies by a certain date, she can usually estimate how long her people will have to work in order to achieve the target. This makes the job a bit less stressful than is true when you are trying to predict how long a project will take when there is no history available.

## It's Not Just Scheduling!

The most important *misconception* about project management is that it is just scheduling. Certainly the schedule is a major tool of managing a project, but having a software program that does project scheduling does not make a person a project manager. In fact, before we go too far, we should really ask what we mean by *managing!*

> Project management is not just scheduling!

The most common definition that I have seen is that *managing is getting work done through other people.* There is a basic core truth in this, but I don't think it goes far enough. I believe that a manager has a lot more to do than this. Managers not only need to get work done; they must also determine what needs to be done in the first place! They should be doing this with a clear understanding of the organization's overall purpose or mission, current environmental realities, future trends, and so on. They must clearly be extremely *proactive*, rather than sitting around waiting for something to happen. If a manager waits until his supervisor tells him what to do, then simply passes the orders along to his own subordinates, he is getting work done through other people, but he is really not much more than a link in a communications network, and that is not my idea of managing.

> Managing is the application and controlling of scarce resources to achieve desired organizational objectives, including survival, adaptation, and growth.

Note that all of this applies to project managers as well as to general managers. It seems to me that a project manager has to do most of the things that general managers do—plus a lot more.

# Achieving Control

The job of any manager is to control the application of scarce resources to achieve organization objectives. However, I don't mean *control* in the old command-and-control sense in which the manager might be heard to say he was going to kick butts to get the job done. Rather, I am using the word *control* in a guidance or information systems way. This definition is shown in the box.

> Control is exercised by comparing where you are to where you are supposed to be, so you can take corrective action when there is a deviation.

This definition leads to an inescapable conclusion—it is your *plan* that tells you where you are supposed to be, so if you have no plan, you have nothing to compare against, so control is impossible!

Unfortunately, there are a lot of forces in American society that encourage us to avoid planning. One is a paradigm problem. We are ready-fire-aim, "just do it" in our focus. We value action that leads to tangible results, and planning doesn't give us that same sense of achieving results, so we devalue it.

> **Paradigm:** a belief or model of what the world is supposed to be like.

A fellow attended one of my project management seminars at the University of Wisconsin-Madison, then came back several months later to my Project Teams class. He said that when he left the first class he was eager to apply what he had learned, so he got his team together to plan their project. His boss came by the meeting room and called him outside.

"What are you doing?" he wanted to know.

"We're planning the project," explained the manager.

"You don't have time for that," said his boss. "Get out there and get the job done."

This is not an uncommon reaction.

The new impediment to planning comes from people who have learned about chaos theory. In chaos theory we find that small perturbations can lead to very large effects. The common example is that a butterfly flaps its wings in California and sometime later the weather changes on the East Coast. Citing this example, some people say that it is a waste of time to plan because there are so many environmental influences that can undo our plans.

There is some truth to this when applied to long-range business planning. As Henry Mintzburg (1989) has said, the fallacy of such long-term plans is that we pretend the world will stand still while we execute them. Since this does not happen, we find that such plans are seldom valid for the entire term, and we spend a lot of time revising them.

Detailed planning may also be wasted on operations or processes that are subject to considerable influence from the environment, where they are poorly defined in the first place. When the argument is extended to short-term or well-defined projects, however, it goes too far. I know of only one author who has correctly addressed this issue. Ralph Stacey, in his book *Managing the Unknowable* (1992), has shown that we need good planning for day-to-day operations, projects, and so on, but that we should not make highly detailed plans for long-range business issues, as they do need revision quite often.

In projects, a major reason that planning is so important is that we find a high level of rework in jobs that are not well planned. In fact, rework can amount to anywhere from 5 to 40 percent of total project effort. At 30 percent, this is equivalent to having one of every three people on the project team just redoing what the other two did wrong. Obviously, if the rework can be eliminated, you have just increased productivity by the same amount.

## Tools for Managing Projects

There are only a handful of tools for managing projects. These include the following:

- Work Breakdown Structures for identifying work, assigning resources, and estimating
- Critical Path, PERT, and Gantt Scheduling
- Failure Mode Effects Analysis for risk management
- Quality Function Deployment for understanding customer requirements
- SWOT (Strengths, Weaknesses, Opportunities, and Threats) analysis
- Force-field analysis for identifying forces that will help or hinder a project
- Earned Value Analysis for tracking progress
- System modeling software for analyzing the effect of variations on schedule

If you are not familiar with these, I suggest that you read one of the books on project planning, scheduling, and control listed in the reading list.

# The Role of the Project Manager

A project manager has to behave a lot like the leader of a jazz band. She selects the melody that the band will play, sets the tempo and key, invites the players, and lets them do their "thing." Clearly this is not a perfect metaphor, but it does illustrate the essence of project leadership. The reason it is not perfect is that good jazz musicians come to the game knowing the rules of jazz. Improvisation does not mean that a player can go off on a completely different course from the rest of the band. He must stay within the confines of the central melodic line. Further, he can't play twelve measures while the rest play nine; nor can he switch to a different key while the rest stay in the original key. It just won't work.

In a project team, however, not everyone has the same understanding, discipline, and training that good jazz musicians have, so more constraints must be placed on team members by the project manager than would be done by a jazz band leader. If, however, they come to the team with good skills in the functions that they have to perform, then the project leader *is* a lot like a jazz band leader—she can give them the freedom to "do their thing" with minimal interference.

Another task that the project leader must perform that the jazz band leader does not have to do is orchestrate the interactions among the members of the team. In the jazz band, these interactions are heard and understood by the musicians. In the project team, no such obvious "visibility" exists, so the project leader must provide that coordination.

Also, a project manager is not necessarily an expert in the technology of the team. This is especially true when the team is multidisciplinary. I myself am an electrical engineer, but I am an analog designer. I am not so familiar with digital electronics. So If I were heading a team doing digital design, I certainly could not direct the digital designers technically. This is even more obvious if you consider that I may have a chemist or an ergonomics expert on the team—both subjects about which I have very little knowledge.

So how do I know if a team member is doing poor-quality work? I don't. I must rely on someone else to advise me. In a matrix organization, I will rely on the person's functional manager. In a pure-project organization, I will rely on an outside person in that discipline to advise me.

## The Need for People Skills

One given in managing projects is that you will always have a lot of responsibility but no authority. This is a common complaint from project managers, and it is likely to stay that way for a long time to come. So how do you get anything done when you have no authority?

To answer this question, consider the situation of a company president. I have asked several of them, "Does your authority (a president certainly has a lot) guarantee that people will do what you want done in your company?" They quickly admit that it does not.

"What does get things done?" I ask.

"Well, in the final analysis, they have to want to do it," the presidents say. "My job is to get them to want to do it."

"Then what good is your authority?" I ask.

They think about this, then say, "It gives me the ability to enforce some sanctions when people don't do what needs to be done, but even these are limited by law."

The conclusion is obvious: Even a company president has to resort to influence in order to get things done. Project managers can expect to do no better. So those people skills are extremely important for a project manager.

Political skills are also important. I have talked to a lot of project managers who say that they spend upwards of 40 percent of their time on political issues. It probably isn't that high on most projects, but there will definitely be some political overhead in any project.

What if you hate that aspect of the job? What should you do? I suggest that you rethink your career and forget about being a manager—project or otherwise. I don't think you will be very good at it if you hate it.

On the other hand, if you are willing to learn the people skills, fine. You definitely can do so. "Even leadership?" you ask.

Yes, even leadership. I was recently talking with a career military officer who told me that when he started his career the military believed that leadership could not be taught. You had to be born with the ability. Now they know differently and do extensive training of officers.

## Test Yourself

1. A Work Breakdown Structure is:
   a. A failure of a team member to complete his work on time
   b. A graphical method of dividing a large project into manageable "chunks"
   c. An organization chart for a project team
   d. A diagram that shows the sequence in which work is done

2. A PERT or CPM diagram is:
   a. Used to keep uninformed members of the team in the dark about what is going on
   b. A diagram using bars to show when tasks should start and end
   c. A diagram that shows the sequence of work with arrows and also determines the critical path through the project
   d. Both b and c

3. A project is defined as:
   a. A one-time job
   b. A task with several people working on it
   c. A repetitive operation
   d. A job with both parallel and sequential tasks

4. Risk analysis is done for the purpose of:
   a. Proving that a project cannot be completed as planned
   b. Showing that Murphy's law is right—if something can go wrong, it will
   c. Assigning a value to our monetary exposure in a project
   d. Identifying those events that could cause serious problems in the execution of a project

5. Quality Function Deployment is used in projects to:
   a. Understand how customer requirements relate to product or service features

    b.  Apply statistical process control to the project work

    c.  Assign probabilities of failure to project tasks

    d.  Estimate costs

6. The most important skills a project manager must have are:

    a.  Math skills

    b.  Technical ability

    c.  Human relations skills

    d.  Coordination skills

The answers are in Appendix A.

# CHAPTER 3

# The Role of the Project Manager

There seems to be confusion among senior managers about just what role a project manager should play in an organization. In fact, some project managers also seem unclear about their role. Unless that role is clear to everyone in the organization, a project manager cannot be very effective. So let's examine that role before getting into teams and team performance.

In Chapter 2 we discussed the fact that project managers often have a lot of responsibility but no authority, and I said that this is likely to be true in the majority of situations. I also pointed out that the importance of authority is overblown, since even company presidents must use influence to get things done.

I believe that the most important point for project managers to understand is that they do have total responsibility for ensuring that every detail of their project is handled properly. This does not mean that the project manager is to micromanage the members of the team, but it does suggest that he or she must be highly proactive, as opposed to reactive.

Too often I find that project managers are practicing little or no follow-up to ensure that things scheduled to be done are actually getting done. For example, a requisition for a purchased part is filled out, signed, and forwarded to the Purchasing Department. The part is needed in two weeks, and the vendor has said that delivery time poses no problem. Two weeks go by and the part has not arrived.

Now panic sets in because the part is critical to the next step in the job, which just happens to be on the critical path! Frantic phone calls soon reveal that the requisition was misplaced in the Purchasing Department and that the order has not even been placed. The only course of action now is to call the vendor to see if shipment can be expedited. It can be but at a significant cost in shipping charges. In addition, the time lost waiting

Exactly what role a project
manager should play in an
organization is sometimes
confusing. Unless that role
is clear to everyone, a project
manager cannot be effective.

for the part must now be recovered through overtime, so members of the team are not happy.

Whose fault is it? Well, we could blame the team member who needed the part for not pressing the issue, but that person will say, "I did my part. I gave a requisition to the project manager. I assumed she was handling everything."

She says the same thing in turn: "It is the fault of the Purchasing Department. They dropped the ball."

Soon a full round of recriminations has taken place, which serves no positive purpose at all. The point is, the part is late, and a price has to be paid to recover from the impact.

I learned a long time ago that no one cares as much about my projects as I do, so it is my responsibility to see that all of this is taken care of. When a requisition is sent to Purchasing, it is easy enough to attach a note saying that the part is needed in two weeks and to ask that the purchasing agent call you with a promised delivery date from the vendor once that is known. If you don't hear anything in a day or so, you call Purchasing and ask what is the status of the order. They may be a little bugged by your calling to check on it, but that's better than dealing with the chaos that results from the ball being dropped.

> **Principle:** No one cares as much about your project as you do.

In the same way, when I know that someone is supposed to start a project task next week, I call ahead of time and ask if he is going to be ready to start on time. It is too late if you wait until the required start date and then learn that he couldn't get to it. If you call ahead of time and find that there is a problem, you may be able to do something about it.

> **Principle:** A major key to success is to practice follow-up and to be highly proactive.

One trap that is insidious is to have people say, "What's the big hurry? I have float in my part of the schedule." Relying on float is a major reason for projects getting into trouble. People take the float at the front end of a task, then, when a problem with the work develops, they can't finish on time.

To help understand this, you have to remember that task durations are always *estimates,* which is just a nice way of saying that they are *guesses,* and those guesses are very uncertain in many cases. So the best operating rule-of-thumb is that float should always be kept in reserve to allow for the unexpected or the fact that the estimate was inaccurate to begin with.

> **Principle:** Float should never be used up at the beginning of a task, but should be kept in reserve to handle the unexpected.

In today's downsized world, it is extremely difficult to get people to follow this rule, but you—as the project manager—must try to convince people of its importance. You may have to plead, cajole, or even twist arms, but it is the only way to achieve some semblance of control over your project.

# Qualities of Project Managers

Every manager in an organization is in some sense a parent to the people reporting to him or her. Like it or not, this is the truth. Naturally, I don't

> **Nurture: 1.** To nourish; feed. **2.** To educate; train. **3.** To help grow or develop; cultivate: *nurture a student's talent.*

mean this in any literal sense, but figuratively, there are a lot of common elements. One of these is nurturing. As the dictionary definition says, to nurture a team member would be to help that person grow or develop. I believe that this is a project manager's responsibility, even when the team is a matrix or cross-functional one. If nothing else, helping each person to become more proactive would be useful.

You should be a coach, mentor, mediator of disputes and conflicts, cheerleader, and even "gopher" when the need arises. Occasionally, you might also be required to do some job counseling, especially if one of your team members has performance problems. Chapter 15 offers more information on how to handle marginal performance.

You are also expected to stand up for your team against anyone who might behave in ways harmful to it. In addition, you are expected to break roadblocks, deal with political issues, and so on.

To create a summary of what is required of a project manager, I have asked people in my classes to list the qualities and skills they think it takes to make a good manager. The following list contains the more significant characteristics suggested by participants.

| | |
|---|---|
| Good listener | Mutual ownership |
| Supportive | Buffer to the rest of the organization |
| Organized | Visible leadership |
| Clears roadblocks | Technical knowledge |
| Mutual respect | Fair |
| Team builder | Flexible |
| Knows own limitations | Open-minded |
| Sense of humor | Delegates |
| Gives feedback | Honest/trustworthy |
| Good decision maker | Understanding |

The most obvious thing about this list is that it is somewhat overwhelming. I don't believe that any single human being can fulfill all these requirements. I know I certainly cannot. So what this means for me is that I have to be aware of those areas in which I excel and those in which I am weak. In those areas of weakness, I need to enlist the support of other members of my team to help me out.

Of course, there are personal attributes that can't be delegated. I need to be honest and trustworthy, for example. If members of the team do not consider me to be honest, then they surely won't trust me, and I will have virtually no influence over them. This means that my job will be nearly impossible.

Likewise, if I lack credibility, I will have difficulty managing the team. This can be particularly hard for managers of multidisciplinary teams. People from disciplines outside your own know that you don't know much about what they do, and this can cause problems. Occasionally, members outside your discipline may take advantage of your ignorance by "sandbagging" their estimates and even doing substandard or poor-quality work.

This is where the functional manager comes in. The role of a functional manager in a matrix project is to evaluate the quality and quantity of work being done for the project by his direct reports and to give them

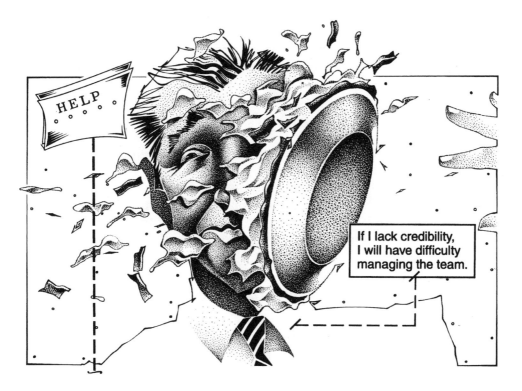

If I lack credibility, I will have difficulty managing the team.

their performance appraisals—with input from the project manager. Naturally, the project manager can't rate them on technical performance but must stick to things like cooperation, communication with others in the team, attention to deadlines, and so on. This is one way to gain loyalty to the project team in a matrix organization.

> **Principle:** It is the functional manager's job to evaluate the quality and quantity of work done by people from his department assigned to a project.

Speaking of functional managers, one highly important aspect of your job as project manager is to build good relationships with these individuals. You don't necessarily have to socialize with them after work to do this. You simply have to get to know them, to know what "makes them tick," and to try to be on good terms with them. The reason is easy to see—if you ever need a favor from a functional manager, you are more likely to get it from someone you are on good terms with. This is discussed in more detail in Chapter 6.

## The Need for Technical Skills

Although I have strong concerns about project managers being "working project managers," meaning that they must do some technical work in technology projects, I do believe that they must have some background in a technical discipline. I have never believed the old adage that "If you're a manager, you can manage anything." I think that has been shown to be a myth long ago.

However, in technology projects (whether in engineering, software, or life sciences), you must be able to understand the issues involved in solving problems. For one thing, you need to support your team; for another, you need to have some feeling for the magnitude of the difficulties team members are facing; and you can't do either of these very well without having some training in the technology yourself.

## Learning to Act

Around 1980, I attended a seminar in management psychology taught by John Grinder, who was a codeveloper of Neuro-Linguistic Programming, a psychological discipline that enjoyed considerable popularity for several years. John suggested that we attend an acting course as a way of developing our management skills. This seemed a bit odd, so John explained that good acting skills are invaluable in many situations.

For example, one of the problems that some managers have is that they do not come across as managers. Something is missing in their self-presentation repertoire. They are not perceived by others as managers because they don't look like managers.

This is akin to John Malloy's suggestion in *Dress for Success* (1993) that a person must dress like a manager to be taken seriously. Through research he showed that certain "uniforms" exist in the business world, and a person who does not wear one of these will not be seen as a manager and will therefore be unable to effectively influence others.

Grinder also explained that there are times when it is useful to be able to look calm on the outside when you are seething underneath and, conversely, that there are times when it helps to look really angry on the outside even though you are calm on the inside. He also pointed out that acting skills give people the ability to be highly flexible in their behavior, and the need for flexibility is supported by the Law of Requisite Variety, which is discussed in more detail in Chapter 4. Just to whet your appetite, this law says that the person in a group with the greatest flexibility in his behavior will control the team. If you are the project leader, this should be you, so developing flexible behavior is very important.

## Understanding Business or Economics

Whether you are a project manager in a business or not-for-profit organization, I believe it is imperative that you understand some basic economics. I have worked with several research labs in which the scientists and / or engineers have no regard at all for financial issues. They work as if the company had an unlimited pot of gold. They refuse to be held accountable for results.

In one company I know of, Corporate told one of its divisions, "For the past several years, you have given us a 4 percent return on our investment. We can get better than that at the bank, and if you don't do better, we are going to divest you and put our money somewhere else." In this very company, many of the technical people worked as if money were no object. Several had been on the job for ten years and had produced nothing of any value for the past five years.

Yet, when confronted with this, they were incredulous: "We're scientists!" they protested. "This is the nature of research."

Not really. A researcher who learns nothing of value in five years is just screwing around. I'm sorry, but that's the way I see it.

The thing we all have to understand is that *the only person who gives you the money that becomes your profits is your customer!* And without profits, you cannot fund research, so if the researchers are not developing ideas that eventually become products, the company will eventually go broke.

We must all be accountable for our performance. So when we insist on tracking project results and engineers howl that they are professionals and should not have to track their time, I'm sorry, I have no patience with them. I recently applied for a trademark, and my attorney sent me a bill itemized in 0.1-hour increments. When I'm paying him $135 an hour, a tenth of an hour is $13.50. I appreciate his being accountable, because I would rather not pay for work done for someone else.

In the same manner, it is common for loaded labor rates in organizations to be $60 to $120 an hour for professionals. I expect them to account for that time.

So what does this have to do with project managers? Plenty. If you don't know the basics of return on investment (ROI), how profits are calculated, what loaded labor rates are, and so on, you need to learn these, because a major aspect of your role as project manager is to think economically. You have to wear the hat of a business-person when you run projects, so that the economic interests of the organization are protected.

## Skills Required of Project Managers

What follows is a general list of the kinds of skills that project managers need. This list might form the basis for a career development program for project managers. Note that it covers the Project Management Institute's Project Management Body of Knowledge (PMBOK) fairly closely.

### Basic Tools of Project Management: Planning, Scheduling, and Control

- Work Breakdown Structures
- Critical Path method
- Earned value analysis

### Advanced Project Management Skills

- Systems thinking
- Principles of quality (TQM)
- Contracting
- Risk management

### People Skills

- Conflict management and resolution
- Team management
- Leadership skills
- Decision making
- Communication
- Negotiation
- Cross-cultural training

### Human Resources

- How to conduct performance reviews
- How to deal with protected-class individuals

### Business Skills

- Cost/project accounting
- Marketing
- Managerial finance
- Economics
- Business ethics

### Other Tools (Depends on Kinds of Projects Managed)

- Analytical hierarchy process
- Quality Function Deployment (QFD)
- Failure Mode Effects Analysis (FMEA)
- General statistics, especially Design of Experiments (DOE)
- Taguchi analysis
- Design reviews
- Scheduling and estimating methods
- Internet navigation

## Assess Yourself

You might want to assess yourself now by answering the following questionnaire and then do so again after you have finished this book. Your score should increase after you have completed the entire book. (If you get 100 percent at this point, you probably don't need to read the book!)

1. I know how to draw a Work Breakdown Structure.      Yes   No
2. I can create a Critical Path or PERT diagram.        Yes   No

3.  I know how to use scheduling software to manage my projects.                                                          Yes   No
4.  I know how to measure progress using earned value analysis.                                                           Yes   No
5.  I have a methodology for managing projects from start to finish.                                                      Yes   No
6.  I can quote the definition of control from memory.                Yes   No
7.  I know how to resolve conflict with another person.               Yes   No
8.  I can be a third-party mediator when conflict exists between other people.                                            Yes   No
9.  I understand the basics of business economics.                   Yes   No
10.  I know how communication affects relationships.                  Yes   No
11.  I have a standard procedure for dealing with marginal employees.                                                     Yes   No
12.  I follow up routinely on tasks to ensure that they are done on time.                                                 Yes   No
13.  I know the essentials of managing team development.              Yes   No
14.  I understand the principles of human motivation.                Yes   No
15.  I understand the implications of the Law of Requisite Variety.                                                       Yes   No

*Scoring:* Give yourself one point for each "Yes" answer. To consider yourself prepared to manage projects, you should have a score of at least 11 points. If you receive less than that number, read the rest of this book!

# SECTION TWO
# Teams and Behavior in Organizations

# CHAPTER 4

# Behavior in Organizations

To understand teams in organizations, it is helpful to understand those aspects of organizations that affect people in general. Of course, to cover this subject thoroughly would be a book in itself, so all I want to do in this chapter is present some of the more important influences on behavior. These then will form a good foundation for understanding team behavior.

## Employment Is an Exchange Relationship

A number of factors enter into a person's decision to accept a job with a company. Will the work be interesting, challenging, and something he can do? Will the people with whom he will work be the kind of people he likes? Is the job site easy to reach? Is the pay acceptable or adequate? What kind of person is his prospective boss?

We could go on and on. Still, in the final analysis, people accept and remain in jobs for one reason: What they must *do* for the organization is well balanced by what they *get* from it. If the exchange is severely imbalanced, they will usually either decline the job or take it only until something better comes along.

> **Principle:** People accept jobs in organizations for one reason: What they expect to *do* for the organization is well balanced by what they expect to *get* from it.

This may sound cold and hedonistic, but it is a basic principle that governs all human relationships: We stay in them so long as there is *something in them for us* that offsets what we have to give to the relationship. Noted psychotherapist Leslie Cameron once told me that when she does marriage counseling, she tries first to determine where the individuals are with respect to what she calls *threshold*. I would call threshold the balance point in the relationship.

She said that if both parties were above threshold, she would do divorce counseling. If they were both below threshold, she would do marriage counseling. The same thing applies to jobs. If a person is above threshold, she will probably look for another job. However, if she is still below threshold, she may be willing to work with her boss to determine what is needed in order to make the job more satisfactory (see Figure 4-1).

As for what a person gets from a job, of course pay is involved, but the employee generally wants more from the organization than just a paycheck. Again, the subject of rewards is a book in itself, but some of the most important organizational rewards include recognition from the boss and one's peers, a sense of achievement, and a feeling that one is making an important contribution through doing meaningful work. As I pointed out in the introduction, surveys have found that many employees feel that they are doing meaningless, mindless jobs. Without a sense of meaning in their jobs, they feel little motivation to work and little commitment to the organization.

In fact, for a long time many managers have behaved as if the only thing that mattered to their employees was a paycheck, with maybe a little recognition thrown in for good measure. For the past thirty or forty years, an annual survey has shown pretty much the same results every time. Managers and supervisors are asked to rank the aspects of their jobs that are important to them. They are also asked to rank items on the list the

**Figure 4-1.** Dissatisfaction threshold in a relationship.

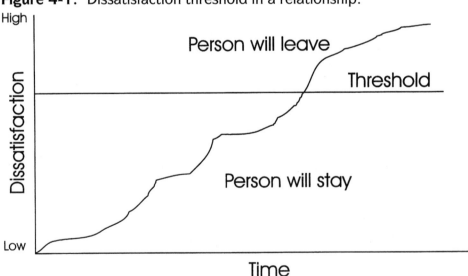

way they think employees would rank them. They generally tend to rank pay very high for employees and lower for themselves. When employees are asked to rank the same items, the results are very similar to the rankings given by supervisors.

What does this mean for you as a project manager? Clearly, a person who is on your project team must experience that assignment as a fair exchange. If not, there will be a lack of commitment and motivation, and the quality of the person's work will likely suffer. Your job, as project manager, is to ensure that the exchange is equitable for both the employee and your project. If you experience deficits in the performance of a team member, you need to find out whether it is because the person lacks ability

or motivation. We will discuss this diagnostic process in greater detail in Chapter 15, but, for now, suffice it to say that if the person is competent, then any performance deficit may be caused by lack of motivation, and this lack of motivation may be because the person does not consider the exchange adequate.

How are you going to determine if this is the case? Talk to her. Ask her what she expects from the job. If you can correct the situation, do so. If you can't, see if you can find another person to trade places with her. Or, if no options exist, you may both have to just grin and bear it for the duration of the project. It's not a perfect world—for any of us.

# Motivation: The Mystery and Myth

As I mentioned previously, many managers think that employees are motivated only by pay. It seems to me that unless you understand motivation, you simply cannot be effective as a manager.

> **Principle:** People are motivated to behave in ways that will satisfy their internal needs, wants, or concerns.

There are a number of theories of motivation, and you can find countless books on the subject. What you will find is that they all boil down to a basic principle: People are motivated to behave in ways that will satisfy their internal needs, wants, or concerns. Since these cover an endless spectrum, it is easy to be confused by what motivates someone and what doesn't.

The most important point is that motivation always comes from *within* a person, not from outside. You can't provide it. There must be an internal drive to do something. You can arouse this, but that is all. For example, I have met a number of people who enjoy climbing cliffs for sport. They all tell me that occasionally they get into a tight spot and wonder what they are doing there, but once they have succeeded in climbing this particular cliff, they forget their fears. In fact, when a friend later invites them to climb another cliff, they say, "I can't wait to see if I can do it."

> **Principle:** All motivation comes from *within* a person. The term *external motivator* is a misnomer.

To me, this is what is meant by true motivation. The person has an internal drive to climb cliffs, and all you have to do is arouse it. If the drive does not exist, you will find it difficult or even impossible to instill it. For example, I have vertigo pretty badly, so you are not going to entice me to climb a cliff, even if you offer me a million dollars. On the other hand, I have numerous drives of my own, so if you offer me a chance to satisfy one of those, I am ready to participate. Further, it is true that I must be paid for my work so that I can pay my bills, but most of my work involves truly motivating activities that are rewarding in and of themselves.

## Demotivators: The Other Side of the Coin

What some managers don't realize is that there is another factor to consider in the motivation equation. People can be *turned on* by being able to satisfy their internal needs; they can also be *turned off* by certain aspects of the job situation. In fact, I often say that organizations have more problems of demotivation than of motivation. That is, they are doing so many things to turn people off that they never experience motivated employees. If they

> **Principle:** A person can't be turned on and turned off at the same time. Being turned off takes priority over being turned on.

just quit their negative practices, motivation would (in most cases) take care of itself.

To illustrate, the loss of a loved one is perhaps the most powerful demotivator there is. A person who has just experienced such an event will have almost no drive to perform job duties, no matter how attractive these functions would be under better conditions. In a less extreme sense, an employee who is in a job situation that contains unpleasant aspects can be expected to suffer a loss of motivation. A common example is that the work itself is so boring that the person can hardly stand it.

I am frequently asked how to get people to want to do such jobs. This questions is really worded as, "How do you get employees to want to do something they don't want to do?" In rare cases, you can actually do this. For instance, suppose I don't want to go to a party. Perhaps I don't like parties very much. But you tell me that Julian Bream (a very excellent classical guitarist) is going to be there, and I change my mind. I *do* want to go to the party now because there is value in the event that I did not know about before.

This, then, is the invariable principle: If you can show the person that there is some valued payoff for doing a task, then you may change her attitude toward it. To use a crude example, cleaning toilets is not something many of us look forward to doing. However, if someone says to me, "Think how important it is to your family that the toilets be clean," then I will want to clean the toilets for the benefit of my family. Note, however, that I probably won't *like* cleaning toilets; I am simply doing it because of a sense of duty and caring for my family. Further, I may not really enjoy that party, but I will enjoy meeting Julian Bream.

I think the key here is to differentiate between gaining *compliance* and getting someone to *want* to do something. We sometimes comply with

directives in the organization without really wanting to do the task itself. Unfortunately, compliance is not very satisfying over the long range, whereas performing motivating activities is. Whenever possible, a manager should try to use motivating factors with team members rather than simply gaining their compliance.

# Helping Team Members to Find Meaning in Their Work

One of the most insidious demotivators in jobs is work that is considered meaningless by the employee. As I related earlier, studies have found that many American workers consider their work to be meaningless. The first responsibility of any manager is, I believe, to try to show team members how their part of the job contributes to the whole and why it is important. You may say, "Oh, isn't that obvious?"

> **Principle:** For work to be motivating, it must have *meaning* for the worker.

Maybe.

But I wouldn't take it for granted. After all, the project manager should have a perspective on the entire project that a team member may lack. So take the time to explain why the entire project is important and how each individual's part fits in.

I am not talking here from a theoretical point of view. I am talking from experience. In about the third year of my career as an engineer, the company I worked for was experiencing hard times. We were in a recession and were forecasting a drop in sales that year from around $2.5 million to around $2 million. That is a huge percentage loss, and we knew that we were facing drastic cost-cutting measures if we couldn't find a way to get sales back up. Part of that cost cutting certainly would have been a layoff.

Then an opportunity dropped into our laps. A request for quotes was received from a large government agency in South America. By coincidence, the total sale was worth about $500,000, almost exactly what we needed to maintain our annual sales volume.

As part of the proposal, we were required to provide equipment for evaluation by the government. This involved making some minor design and cosmetic changes in our radio equipment. The nomenclature on the panels also had to be changed from English to Spanish, and we had to provide literature in Spanish.

I was given the job of making all of this happen in a very short time frame. The people assigned to help me were drawn from various departments, and none of them reported to me directly—it was a typical "dotted-line" relationship—meaning that I had no authority over any of them. I should also add that at this point in my career I knew nothing about the theory of teams. All I had was the belief that I should try to treat people the way I liked to be treated.

So I got them all together and explained the situation. I told them how important the job was and said that I was really counting on all of them to do their part. I was there to help them whenever I could and to coordinate their efforts, but that was all. I was not the *boss* in any sense of the word. I also explained the reality of the situation—that layoffs were imminent if we couldn't get sales up. I don't like using negatives to energize people, but in this case I believed that telling the truth was necessary.

For the next couple of months, we all worked incredibly hard. We put in ten to twelve hours a day Monday through Friday, eight hours on Saturday, and occasionally a few hours on Sunday. All voluntarily, all without complaining.

One morning I was in the engineering lab about 7:45 A.M., and a woman who was preparing Spanish literature for the project came to me, handed me a stack of papers, and said, "Here is your literature. I'm going home and going to bed."

I did a bit of a double take, so she said, "I knew if I didn't get these done by this morning, you were going to miss your deadline, so I stayed out here all night and finished them, so now I'm going to get some sleep."

I hadn't asked her to do this. She had done it on her own, and for only one reason—she knew how important the job was. This is the power of *meaning* in the workplace. Take care of this and you will have dedicated, committed employees. Treat people as if they don't need to know why something must be done and you will have robots for employees.

## How Systems Affect Behavior

Another factor that can have a significant effect on employee behavior is the organizational system itself. In his book *The Fifth Discipline* (1990), Peter Senge describes a business simulation that was developed to teach people how systems affect them. It is called the Beer Game. The scenario is that a small brewery produces a beer called Love Beer. It isn't a big seller. A typical convenience store will normally sell only about four cases a month.

Then sales of Love Beer take off like a rocket. People start coming into the convenience stores and ordering Love Beer like it was the greatest thing going. In no time at all, convenience stores all over town have sold out, and people are clamoring for more beer. The stores soon learn the reason for the big demand. A song has hit the airwaves that mentions Love Beer, and now everyone wants to try it.

Naturally, merchants are quick to recognize a good thing and don't want to lose sales, so the stores start ordering large quantities of Love Beer from their distributors. Because this is going on all over town, the distributors are soon out of stock. They, in turn, call the brewery and tell the people there to get busy and send them more beer. The tiny brewery is overwhelmed. They can't keep up with demand working normal hours, so they ask people to work overtime. Soon they realize that even overtime won't enable them to keep up, so they start hiring people to work a second shift.

Then disaster strikes.

The novelty of the song and the beer wear off, and demand drops back to its original level. Now the stores have excess inventory, and they start calling their distributors to cancel unfilled orders. The distributors do the same with the brewery. The brewery management then has to lay off all those people they've just hired for the second shift, and they are stuck with a large quantity of raw materials with which to make beer.

Senge says that they have played this game around the world, with people from all walks of life and all kinds of educational backgrounds, and they always get the same result. This leads to an obvious conclusion: *The system itself can be said to generate the behavior, regardless of the people involved!* When behavior is caused by the system, if you want to change that behavior, you have to change the system.

> **Principle:** Your organizational systems must support the desired behavior. If this is not the case, change the system before trying to change the person!

The same point was also made by Dr. Deming, using a bowl of beads. The bowl contained a mix of red and white beads, with 10 percent being red beads. These red beads were considered to be "bad." People from the audience were asked to insert a paddle drilled with a matrix of holes into the bowl so that the beads would adhere to the holes. The number of red beads was recorded as "defects," and all the beads were returned to the bowl, keeping the population ratio constant at 10 percent red beads. This procedure was repeated a number of times and percentages of "defects" were recorded.

Then group members were asked what they thought the average percentage defective would be when the data were analyzed. They unanimously said, "10 percent." Deming challenged them to explain their answer. "Because the population contains 10 percent red beads," they said. "What difference does that make?" Deming challenged. They then tried to use the Central Limit Theorem as an answer, and Dr. Deming rejected it.

Finally, he pointed out that the result depends on the paddle used. He explained that he had several paddles, one that would settle down to an average of 9.8 percent, another at 10.2 percent, and a third at exactly 10 percent. Then he hit them with the real meaning of all this: We have given "workers" a process that will inherently produce a certain average defectiveness level, regardless of how they go about it. If you want to achieve "zero defects," you have to change the process to one that is capable of achieving that result. Otherwise, you can admonish people to "do it right the first time," and it will only cause frustration, as the workers know that they have been set up (Walton, 1986).

In a similar fashion, we set up project managers and team members for failure. When a team is expected to meet its targets in a system that is starved for resources, and we respond to failure with "no excuses," then team members quickly realize that they are powerless to affect the outcome. If project teams are to achieve desired results, we must ensure that the systems in which they work are capable of the performance levels we expect. If not, then we must change the system.

This is clearly illustrated in an article that appeared in the March–April 1996 issue of the *Harvard Business Review*. It is entitled "Getting the Most Out of Your Product Development Process" and was written by Adler, Mandelbaum, Nguyen, and Schwerer. The authors studied a number of companies and wrote a case study based on their findings. What they found was that it often takes five times longer to get product development projects completed than the Critical Path schedule predicts (as computed by scheduling software). The reasons are many, but they boil down to system problems. Companies take on too many projects for the capacity they have. They constantly change priorities on projects, causing team members to be jerked around from one job to another. They base estimates on guesswork rather than historical data. And so on.

It might be tempting to think that only product development projects suffer from these maladies, but more and more companies are reporting similar findings in all kinds of environments. These system problems must be addressed if project managers are to be held accountable for results, and those system issues must generally be handled by senior managers. The responsibility that project managers have is to make management aware of the problems and to suggest solutions. We will discuss some of these solutions later.

# The Law of Requisite Variety

For managers, the Law of Requisite Variety is probably the most important principle for systems theory. Clearly a manager is supposed to be in control, in the sense of ensuring that project objectives are achieved. She has the responsibility and accountability for seeing that it is so.

What the Law of Requisite Variety tells us is that the team member with the greatest variability in his behavior will control the system. If that person is not the team leader, then she (the team leader) will lose control of the project. For

> **Principle:** In any system of humans or machines, the element in the system with the greatest variability in its behavior will control the system.
>
> —Ross Ashby

instance, if a member of the team uses up all the float available to his activity, he is on the critical path, and if he slips any more, that slip will cause the end date for the project to slip accordingly. Another way to say this is that if any member of the team goes out of control, then eventually this might affect the entire project.

What, then, is the project manager to do? The law says that she must have more flexibility in her behavior than that exhibited by the system. So there are two options:

1. Increase her flexibility to match or exceed that of the team, or
2. Reduce the variability in team behavior to a level that she *can* match.

Most people think that they have great flexibility in their behavior. And perhaps they do. However, there are limits. Consider this: Have you ever met a person you just couldn't deal with effectively? You tried all kinds of ways of dealing with this person, but nothing worked. In that case, you lacked the flexibility to deal effectively with this person.

Parents sometimes have this problem with their children. No matter what they try, the child continues to behave in some undesirable way. And all the time the parent thinks, "If I could just find the right approach, I could get through to Johnny." And this is probably true.

Actually, much of parenting is aimed at teaching children *rule-governed* behavior that will reduce the range of their behavior to acceptable social limits. In fact, children who are not taught such rules become problem children and eventually problem adults in society. The net result of

such rule-governing is to reduce the variability in the child's behavior so that parents can match his or her behavior, thus permitting them to gain some semblance of control.

We try to do the same thing in organizations. We establish policies and procedures designed to limit the behavior of organization members to acceptable limits. I call this a *negative* approach to reducing variability. Unfortunately, the stimulus for such policies is often the fact that some clown did something stupid; rather than deal with the offender directly, we write a policy telling all organization members that such behavior is unacceptable and will be punished. The problem with this approach is that it does not achieve the desired result, which is to govern behavior. In the first place, most members of the organization didn't need to be told, and in the second, the policy won't stop the clown who chooses to violate it. All the policy really does is exonerate the organization from legal liability if the violator hurts herself.

There is a way to reduce variability in the behavior of team members in a positive way rather than a negative one. That is through proper project planning and practicing empowerment of team members. When team members participate in planning a job, they automatically limit their behavior to activities that are mutually agreed upon. Further, deviations from those planned steps are noted and corrective action taken through the standard project control system.

> **Principle:** Variability in the team should be reduced by good planning, not through "thou shalt not" pronouncements.

Note that even when you take positive steps to limit the variability in team behavior, you still need to work on increasing the flexibility of your own behavior. That is what life-long learning is all about. The more tools you have in your behavioral tool kit, the better able you will be to handle the myriad people and situations you will face throughout your career. In fact, that is really what a book like this is all about—providing you with more techniques (tools) that you can use to deal with those situations.

# The Actor-Observer Attribution Bias— and How to Avoid It

We go through life trying to make sense of the world. In particular, we are concerned about the causes of behavior—both our own and that of others. Did Paul behave in a certain way because of his basic nature or because of something in the situation he was in? Naturally, this is the kind of question managers are always asking about the people who report to them.

For example, in judging employee performance, if a person succeeds or fails at an assignment, we want to know was it because of (1) effort? (2) ability? (3) luck? or (4) task difficulty?

Studies have found that we are inclined to punish able individuals who fail at a task because they didn't try very hard. Cross-cultural studies have also found that parents in the United States make different attributions for their children's failures than Asian parents do. An American parent is likely to say that the child failed because the work was too difficult, whereas an Asian parent will say that the child didn't try hard enough. Now, since task difficulty is a function of one's ability, saying that the

child failed because the task was too hard is equivalent to saying that the child lacked the ability to do the work. Lack of ability is pretty hard to overcome, whereas not trying hard enough is easy to deal with. The child simply has to work harder! (Stevenson, 1992; Stevenson & Stigler, 1992).

In work settings, we find that managers tend to attribute employee failure to some factor in the person. That is, the employee either lacks the ability or didn't try hard enough, or perhaps didn't understand the assignment. Employees, on the other hand, are most likely to attribute their failures to some *situational* factor—the resources were not available, there were too many meetings, and so on. Some managers see this as an attempt to absolve oneself of responsibility for the failure. This difference in attributions naturally leads to conflict between the employee and the manager.

> **Principle:** Managers tend to attribute problems in employee performance to the employee rather than look for a possible systemic cause.

There are several possible explanations for this difference in attributions. For the employee, the most salient influences on her behavior are various aspects of the work situation. From the manager's perspective, the most obvious factor in the job is the employee. The manager sees the employee behaving, does *not* see the situational influences, and says, "She behaved that way because she has certain attributes." The employee says, "I behaved this way because *this* was going on in the situation."

As we have seen, systems do indeed exert a strong influence on employee behavior, so the employee is sometimes telling it like it is. There *was* something in the situation that caused the failure. The lesson here is that managers need to be aware of their tendency to "blame" the person for failure, and employees need to be aware that they tend to look outside themselves for explanations, thus failing to learn when they were unsuccessful because of something they actually did or did not do.

### Apply What You Have Learned

1. During the next week or so, pay attention to the working environment of your team. See if any of the following demotivators exist. If they do, try to take steps to remove those under your control and lobby with higher-level managers to remove the rest.
   - ☐ Poor working conditions (noisy, uncomfortable, lacking in privacy)

☐ Bad relationships among workers or between workers and their supervisors
☐ Company policies that are viewed as unfair
☐ Feelings of being low-status employees (because of how they are treated)
☐ Job insecurity (e.g., layoff imminent, merger plans)

2. When one of your team members has problems, do you attribute the cause to him? Are there any organizational factors (system issues) that could cause his problems? Can you correct any system problems that exist?

3. Have you explained to team members why this project is important—both to the company and to them? If not, take time to do so. Further, explain to each of them how his or her contribution affects the "big picture." If necessary, take them to visit customers, suppliers, or anyone else so that they can see for themselves the importance of the project.

4. Are you trying to reduce team variability through "thou shalt not" pronouncements? If so, try to replace them with good plans. This will reduce variation because each person will have a clear understanding of what he or she is supposed to be doing.

5. To increase your own flexibility as a manager, try new approaches to dealing with people and situations. Do you find some people hard to deal with? Or some situations extremely frustrating? Try imagining yourself dealing successfully with them. There is a principle in psychology that you must be able to see yourself doing something before you can actually do it. Imagine a number of alternative approaches. Then try them.

6. Buy copies of *The 7 Habits of Highly Effective People* by Stephen Covey and give one to each member of your team. Take an hour each week (after work, if necessary) to discuss a chapter together. Try to apply Covey's habits at work and at home.

# CHAPTER 5

# Chaos, Fractals, and Project Teams

In her book *Leadership and the New Science* (1994), Margaret Wheatley suggests that we should rethink the concept of leadership based on what science has taught us about the universe over the past ninety years. As I pointed out in the Preface, we have been taught to see the world around us in terms of Newtonian physics, which treats the world as a machine. Machines can be understood in terms of their parts and structures. By understanding all of a machine's parts, we can understand the entire mechanism. Newtonian thinking leads to reductionism—the attempt to reduce every complex thing to its constituent parts so that these can be understood, and so the entire machine can be understood as well.

Machines also can be thought of as having rigid control mechanisms, governors, and so on. This leads to the belief that long-term planning is perfectly valid in that the long-term behavior of machines is completely predictable. We know, for example, what position the earth should be in a hundred years from now, although some error may be introduced because we cannot model every single influence, e.g., from asteroids.

> **Reductionism:** the attempt to reduce a complex thing to its constituent parts, and to understand the whole by understanding its parts.

Because of this mind-set of seeing everything as a machine, we have viewed organizations accordingly and have designed them as machines. We have even viewed human beings this way, I believe. At best, we are living organisms governed by a brain that is largely a collection of chemical or electrochemical processes. If we could just understand that big lump of gray matter called the brain, then we could completely understand human behavior.

Quantum physics, however, has revealed that the Newtonian model falls apart at the atomic level, and has caused many physicists to question our model of the world at the macro level, that is, at sizes above the atomic. Perhaps the world is not a big clockwork machine that is predictable after all.

In addition to quantum theory, we have developed new branches of mathematics that deal with chaos theory, self-organizing systems, and fractal geometry, all of which have made contributions to computer technology and are also making us rethink what we know about systems. One of the favorite sayings of chaos theory is that if a butterfly flaps its wings in California, this action will eventually affect the weather on the East Coast. The essence of this example is that tiny perturbations can cause large swings in behavior of whatever they affect. For instance, the behavior of a small group of stock buyers might cause the entire market to crash. Or the behavior of one individual might cause an entire organization to fail.

In the case of fractal geometry, we find that very beautiful, complex geometric designs can be built up from the repetition of a single tiny element. This is true of ferns, as seen in Figure 5-1.

**Figure 5-1.** How complex patterns are built from tiny fractals.

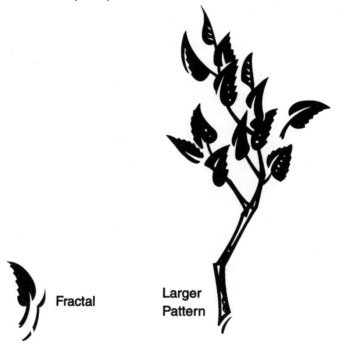

Dr. Wheatley shows how these new principles might affect organizations. For example, in quantum physics we find that as soon as you observe an atomic process, you change it. This principle has, indeed, been found to apply to groups of humans. In the very process of observing group behavior, you change it. This makes it very difficult to obtain valid data on how groups behave. We sometimes try to avoid the effect by having observers watch through one-way mirrors, but even this does not work entirely because the very presence of the mirror tells the members of the group that they might be under observation, and they will then behave differently than usual.

From Dr. Wheatley's book, I have borrowed a handful of ideas that I think can be applied to project teams. These will be discussed in the following text. I encourage you to read her book for a fuller treatment of the connections she makes.

## The Need for Vision and Mission

The words *vision, mission,* and *purpose* have connotations that cause many people to feel a bit ill when they hear them. The simple reason is that they have been so abused and misused. As Karl Albrecht writes in his book *The Northbound Train* (1994, p. viii),

> *In twenty years of working with organizations of almost every imaginable type, I've seen relatively few really powerful and meaningful corporate statements of vision, mission, or philosophy. Most are either vague, puffy, and meaningless, or dull, prosaic, and uninspiring. A very few actually have the power to move people.*

Echoing this sentiment, a participant in one of my seminars said, "Mission statements have been totally discredited."

My response was that the kind he had seen were certainly discredited, but this does not mean that a properly written mission statement is not necessary. I don't believe that any individual or team can be successful without a clear sense of direction, and both the mission and vision provide that direction.

> **Principle:** If you don't know where you're going, how will you know when you get there? A mission statement says where the team is going.

The main point of this, however, is that it is not enough for the team leader to have a mission and vision in his or her head. That mission and vision must be *shared* by all members of the team. I constantly remind people in my seminars that the purpose of planning is not just to produce large Critical Path diagrams and other documents. It is to ensure that we have achieved a *shared understanding* of what the team is trying to do and how it is going to go about it. As Dr. Wheatley says, we are not talking about

> **Principle:** A major purpose of project planning is to produce a shared understanding of where the team is going and how it is going to get there.

visionary leadership but about a shared vision that will drive and guide the team even if the leader takes a false step.

Now what exactly do we mean by vision? Certainly we should differentiate it from the wishful thinking or hallucinations that we sometimes indulge in. So let us begin by considering one aspect of how the mind works. It turns out that until you can "see" yourself doing something, the chances are you will never do it. In fact, psychologists discovered years ago that the mental rehearsal of sports moves, music, speeches, and so on was almost as effective as actual physical rehearsal. Based on this finding, Robert Fritz (1989) has written that everything in this world is created twice—once in the imagination and then again in the tangible, objective world.

As an example of this, let's say that you want to rearrange the furniture in your living room. You try different arrangements in your mind, trying to visualize what each one would look like. You may even sketch the arrangements on paper before you select one. Then you try the actual physical move. It doesn't always come out as you had imagined. Some of us are better than others at visualizing. But at least you are trying.

In the same way, if you are going to design a product, you begin by imagining what it will look like. When I worked in product development, I imagined the outer and inner appearance of the radios I intended to design, including how they would function, how access to various parts would be achieved, and so on. Naturally, my pictures usually evolved over time, because I would find that something didn't work exactly as I had imagined it would, or because I had new insight into how to improve the design. But the image was my starting point, and without that vision I would never have produced anything of consequence!

My job as project leader, of course, was then to communicate that vision to my entire team so that everyone knew exactly what the product was supposed to be like when we finished it. This is not easy to do and is especially hard when you are dealing with something intangible. For example, what does software "look like"? You can't visualize the software

exactly, but you can visualize what it is supposed to do for you. Perhaps it would be correct to say that although an actual visual image is not always possible, a conceptual grasp of what one is trying to create is.

# Information

Information is power, as we all know. Those "in the know" have an advantage over those who are "in the dark." In fact, this is why managers who want to maintain power over others keep information to themselves. We call this mushroom management: Keep them in the dark, feed them a lot of garbage, then, when they grow up, cut them off at the knees and can them.

Fortunately, this tactic almost always backfires on the person who uses it. To see why this is true, consider the difference between a task and an objective. Project leaders sometimes give people tasks to perform without telling them what the objective is. Then, when such people encounter a problem, they can't respond directly. I sometimes fall into this trap myself even though I have known better for a long time.

To illustrate, I had a training program scheduled with one of my regular clients. This client had made my hotel reservations and set up the facility for the program. Then another client from the same city called and asked when I would be in town again. "Two weeks from now," I said. "Great, can you come by and see us for a day?" I told him I could, then, being very busy at the moment, I asked my wife to call the secretary who had made my hotel reservations and tell her to extend my stay by one more night. I then left for an out-of-town trip. When I called home that evening, I found that my request had precipitated total confusion. When my wife asked the secretary to extend the reservation, she said, "Oh, is the program four days duration? We thought it was three."

"I don't know," said my wife. "He didn't tell me anything but to extend the reservation."

Naturally, had I explained to her what was going on, that is, told her the purpose of extending the reservation, she could have answered the question and there would have been no confusion. She needed proper information!

In his book *Thriving on Chaos* (1987, p. 284), Tom Peters writes, "There is no limit to what a properly trained, properly informed, and empowered employee can contribute to a company." I submit that without proper training and information no one can be empowered in the first place. But I strongly agree with Peters that empowerment is an absolute necessity if our teams are to succeed, as I pointed out in Chapter 4. If we are going to err, we should err on the side of giving people too much, rather than too little, information.

> **Principle:** Without information, you are employing hands, not heads. Only with adequate information can people make sound decisions and work independently.

It turns out that information is the "stuff" that feeds many self-organizing systems. Such systems are sort of the opposite of chaotic processes. The term *self-organizing system* is used to describe what happens when seemingly random events arrange themselves in such a way that a pattern is formed. As an example, a few settlers moved to certain areas of North America in the colonizing period. Over time, their randomly dispersed cabins ceased to be random. Instead, they formed orderly patterns around streets, rivers, and other natural landmarks. This is easy to see from the standpoint of security, ready access to resources (such as water), and the need to be able to communicate easily. In fact, the need for information to be shared (communicated) became a major source of the eventual organizing patterns.

Perhaps one of the best defenses against destructive chaos (commonly called bedlam) is good information, which leads to self-organization. I suggest that any team that is to be effective must have free-flowing information of the *right kind* at the *right time.* In fact, Marvin Patterson, former vice president of product development at Hewlett-Packard, has suggested a JIT (Just-in-Time) model for information in product development (Patterson, 1993). That is, if we can deliver needed technical information to a product developer just at the time she needs it, that will make her job most efficient.

## Relationships

I have already pointed out that systems should not be looked at as machines that we try to understand in terms of parts. Rather, a complex system must be understood as a collection of *relationships.* If relationships are healthy, the system will be healthy, and vice versa.

Rather than trying to design rigid command-and-control machine systems, Dr. Wheatley has suggested that we consider creating organizational structures that might facilitate relationships and

> **Principle:** A system can only be understood as a function of the *relationships* among its parts, not just the parts themselves.

then watch what happens. Generally, something useful will happen if we link up the right people, units, and tasks. This is owing to that self-organizing principle of information.

# Fractals

We have already seen that a fractal is a tiny element that can be built up to form a beautifully complex design or pattern. The question is, what would a fractal be in an organization and how would we use it? It turns out that the analog of a fractal element is a *value*.

> **Principle:** Values form the basis by which systems organize themselves. Clarifying a team's values is one way to help pull people together.

Now a value is simply something that is important to us. We have heard a lot in the past few years about changing societal values. And considerable concern has been expressed about the breakdown in values. There is a reason for this. Although we are not always conscious of it, we know intuitively that shared values provide order in a society that would otherwise be chaotic. Values are the raw material from which we derive rule-governed behavior. If people are not individually rule-governed, we have a situation that can lead to a total breakdown of society.

For example, we have learned over the centuries to value life. Thus we have laws forbidding killing, and if you infringe them, there is a severe penalty for such behavior. We are taught to respect the individual and his or her rights, which means that we are not supposed to steal from people, cheat them, lie to or about them, or otherwise harm them.

Undoubtedly, there has been a decline in our values over the past fifty years. A large percentage of the American population has become narcissistic—interested only in themselves. Such people do not respect the rights of others. As Stephen Covey phrases it in *The 7 Habits of Highly Effective People* (1990), we have a character problem in the United States. And this shows up in our teams.

People who are only concerned about me, me, me are more likely to be destructively competitive than cooperative. They run over anyone who gets in their way in their drive for success, which is defined as getting whatever they are after. And if hard work doesn't get them what they're after, they won't hesitate to lie, cheat, or steal to get their way. They also delight in back stabbing to beat their competition. Such behavior inside a team will ultimately destroy that team.

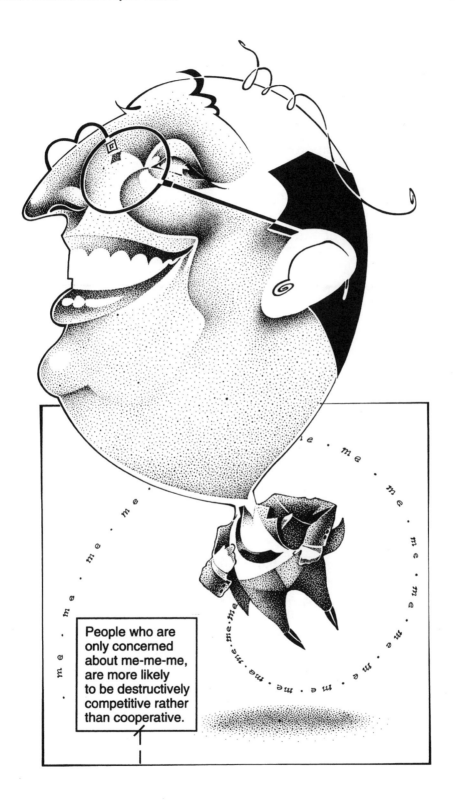

People who are only concerned about me-me-me, are more likely to be destructively competitive rather than cooperative.

Another value that has special relevance to teams is that of honesty. If we are honest with each other, we can trust one another. If we are dishonest, trust is destroyed. When someone lies to us, we learn not to trust him. If he cheats or tries to take something from us that is rightfully ours, we cannot trust him. And a team in which people can't trust each other can hardly be effective, because lack of trust prohibits cooperation.

It is extremely important that a team clarify its values as a conscious exercise. One such approach is presented at the end of this chapter. If you have ever been part of or even just visited an organization with a strong sense of values, you know how powerful, invigorating, and wholesome that climate is. You may not be able to achieve such an effect on an organization-wide basis, but you can do it for your team.

# Applying New Science to Project Teams

Now it is time to apply new science to our project teams. Petzinger (1997) has suggested that we can take advantage of what we have learned about self-organizing systems by doing the following: You have your first meeting with team members. Together you agree on a mission for the team that everyone can buy into. Then as people pursue their daily routines, you encourage them to experiment, to make messes, to seek information and assistance from whatever sources their noses lead them to—all in search of new ways to keep the mission alive. Meanwhile, you create streams of performance data so that people can see what is working. Instead of driving ambiguity and instability out of the workplace, you embrace them.

## Identity

"Identity," according to Stephanie Marshall, "is the principle that is most fundamental to all self-organizing systems. It encompasses the organization's meaning, purpose, and intentionality and provides the coherence around which system stability emerges" (Marshall, 1997, p. 185). Identity helps teams achieve order and transformation, even in turbulent environments, because it provides a constant frame of reference for integrity and renewal. People have the capacity for achievement as a team when the team's identity, purpose, and meaning are clear and when leaders create the right conditions.

One of these conditions is for the leader to bring the team together to think about itself and to make decisions for itself *as a system*. This does not mean that all team decisions should be made by consensus, but it does mean that work on tasks must be set aside occasionally so that people can think about who they are as a team and what they are about.

As Petzinger suggested, the team leader should also involve everyone in the team in creating the team's mission and purpose statement, expounding its values and beliefs, and organizing around them. Even though the mission might be assigned to the team by senior management, working through the writing of a final statement ensures that every member of the team has a *shared understanding* of that mission, which I believe is of the utmost importance if a team is to be successful.

Team leaders should periodically work with every individual on the team to show how each member is connected to the future of the team and to the organization as a whole. In doing so, they can promote a team consciousness and a sense of having a higher purpose. This may sound "touchy-feely," but, as I have mentioned earlier, all employees want to feel that they are contributing to a significant purpose in doing their jobs.

The leader should ensure that decisions made by the team are based on a strong sense of the overall organization's identity. This is in line with physicist David Bohm's dictum to "think globally, act locally."

## Information

Alvin Toffler and others have written about the nature of information as power. This can be used in a positive or negative way. When information is shared with members of a team, it is empowering for the entire group. On the other hand, when a member of the team or the team leader keeps information to himself that could be useful to the entire team, this is negative, a personal use of information for the power it gives.

Information is a dynamic process that becomes the basis for the self-organization of human systems. Without a constant flow of information, systems become closed and isolated. In *Thriving on Chaos* (1987), Tom Peters has written that there is no limit to what a properly trained, informed, and empowered employee can contribute to an organization. My personal view is that without training and information, no one can be empowered in the first place, so a leader's job is to see that all members of a project team have the right information when they need it. If you are going to make a mistake with the dissemination of information, make it in the direction of giving the team too much, rather than too little, information.

Leaders should create multiple pathways for communication and make sure that they are kept open. They should constantly generate and share new knowledge and promote open dialogue, feedback, and interaction among members of the team.

Margaret Wheatley suggests that we should seek out information that surprises us, information that is complex and ambiguous. Team leaders should take a leading role in this and encourage team members to discuss and use such information.

## Relationships

Neuroscience has found that the brain is a neural network, and we can understand relationships as the neural network of a team or organization. Relationships build the organization's capacity for achieving its objectives. Unless all team members feel connected to the organization and its purpose, they cannot identify with its purpose or use information for growth. Gregory Bateson (1980) has said that we must learn to see *patterns* in the world around us, for it is only by understanding these patterns that we can understand our world. Relationships form one of the most important patterns of all.

Leaders must create networks of communication and interaction. They should promote open access to everyone in the system, breaking down political barriers that would inhibit such access. As Dan Dimancescu (1992) has termed it, we want to create a *seamless enterprise.*

Project leaders should help all members of the team to realize that there is strength in the diversity of ideas, which is certain to be a facet of a cross-functional team. Unfortunately, we sometimes feel threatened by diverse points of view, so the team leader's job is to minimize that threat and reframe it as something positive.

A project leader serves as a boundary manager for the team. She should ensure that relationships are developed with other members of the internal organization and with the external environment if necessary, and these relationships should be seen as strategic alliances and partnerships.

Another function for the project leader is to develop a norm for reflection and collective inquiry by the team, as well as a sense of collective accountability. As Margaret Wheatley has said, we could gain great power from one simple practice, which is to ask, after anything significant happens, "What can we learn from this?" We don't need to wait until the formal project review—we can do this at any time and thus promote the actualization of our team as a learning organization.

## In Summary

New sciences are teaching us that the role of the leader is to create the conditions that integrate the three domains of Identity, Information, and Relationships so that our systems can be self-organizing. It is this integration that makes a system synergistic—so that the whole is truly greater than the sum of its parts. And we must abandon the old linear, cause-and-effect models of the past. As Einstein once remarked, "We cannot solve a problem with the same thinking that created it in the first place."

## Exercise: Vision, Information, and Relationships

The following exercise should be done with your entire team. It is best if you can use an off-site location. As the team members answer the questions, post their answers on flip chart pages so they can be reviewed and transcribed later.

1. What is our mission as a team? What are we trying to accomplish? What will that accomplishment *look like* when we have achieved it?
2. Do all members of the team share this vision? If not, what can we do to make sure it is a shared vision? Is it lack of understanding, lack of commitment, or something else?
3. What information do I have that might be useful to others, and how do I best share it?
4. What information do I need to contribute effectively to this team, and how do I obtain it?
5. What blocks the flow of information? How can we remove these blocks?
6. What is the nature of our relationships within the team? With other teams? With suppliers, customers, or senior management? If any of these are "bad," how can we improve them?
7. What are the interests and objectives of team members, other teams, and others with whom we interact? How can we best achieve our objectives without interfering with the objectives of others? In fact, what can we do to ensure that we achieve our objectives while helping others to achieve theirs?
8. What are our values—that is, what is important to us? Make a list of no more than ten key values, as more than that will be unmanageable. What are the things that are so important to us that they are nonnegotiable? What do these values tell us about our behavior, and how should we behave so that these values are maintained?

# CHAPTER 6

# Teams, Herds, and Gaggles of Nerds

If we are to understand and deal effectively with teams, we must have a proper model for doing so. If we begin with a false premise about what teams are like or how they should be, then we can hardly expect to get the desired results from them. For instance, the president of a company once told his staff, "I want everyone on my team to agree with me." That expectation is unlikely to produce good team results.

I think the most important word in any language is *paradigm,* which is defined as a model of reality. It would be more correct to say that a paradigm is our *belief* about what the world is like. We have all formulated beliefs about what the world is like from infancy on to adulthood, and we take these beliefs to be true. Further, we usually behave in ways that make them *seem* true, even if they aren't.

> It's not so much that people don't know that is the problem, but that they know so much that isn't true!
>
> —Mark Twain

As example of this is a person who believes that she is okay but that most other people are no darned good. This outlook is summed up by the expression "I'm okay, you're not okay," from Transactional Analysis (Berne, 1964; Harris, 1969). (The four possible combinations of this expression are shown in Figure 6-1.) Once she has formed this belief, she interacts with people in a hostile, distrustful manner, thereby eliciting from them behavior that confirms what she has believed all along—namely, that they are no good. This is called a self-fulfilling prophecy.

Now, most of us would say that this person has a very sad outlook on the world, and it is unfortunate because most people really are pretty much okay. That is, we consider her outlook to be incorrect or at least

**Figure 6-1.** The four life positions.

| I'm Okay-You're Okay | I'm Okay-You're Not Okay |
|---|---|
| I'm Not Okay-You're Okay | I'm Not Okay-You're Not Okay |

heavily biased. And we see that because of her outlook she has problems with people wherever she goes.

It also turns out that we maintain these beliefs about the world by processing information in such a way that our beliefs are confirmed. For example, the individual who believes that most people are not okay may have someone try to do something nice for her. How do you suppose she will respond? You guessed it. She will wonder what he's up to. She thinks he must be trying to trick her or take advantage of her. Since people are not okay, she reasons, he would not be doing anything nice for her if it weren't for some ulterior motive. This is called *distorting* the meaning of the person's actions.

Or she may not even *notice* that someone is doing something nice for her. She has *deleted* that information from her awareness, so she can continue to say, "No one ever does anything nice for me. People are such rats!"

These two perceptual actions are used by all of us to preserve our cherished beliefs about the world. Of course, not all our beliefs are equally cherished; some are stronger than others. Weaker beliefs can be disconfirmed, and then we do give them up. It is those that have become so ingrained in us that they *practically define who we are as individuals* that are so resistant to being changed.

> **Principle:** We preserve our incorrect beliefs about the world through *deletion* and *distortion*.

One fact is important to remember about paradigms: The map is not the territory. That is, the model never completely captures "reality." We can draw a map of an area, but it will be a representation only. What is really important is that if the map is that of another territory, it can hardly help us get around the one we are in.

> **Principle:** The map is not the territory.

So what does all of this have to do with teams?

As I said at the beginning of this chapter, if we have incorrect paradigms about what teams are like, then we can hardly expect to deal effectively with them. For example, I have heard people apply to teams the expression, "A chain is only as strong as its weakest link." And this is not true.

To see why this is so, look at Figure 6-2. As you can see, if a chain is being used to pull a heavy load, then certainly the weakest link will determine how heavy that load can be before the chain breaks.

> We cannot solve a problem with the same thinking that created it in the first place.
> —Albert Einstein

However, if we examine Figure 6-3, we see that it is different when a team is pulling a load. Now the strength of the "chain" is the *sum total of the strengths of the individuals composing it* so that even the weakest "link" is contributing!

**Figure 6-2.** Chain pulling a load.

**Figure 6-3.** Team pulling a load.

In fact, even this is not an entirely a correct statement, because we find that teams can generate a *synergistic* effect in which the strength of the team is actually greater than the sum of its parts!

Nevertheless, we hear people complain that Howard is not carrying his share of the load, which sometimes means that we expect everyone to carry an equal part of the work, although this is not realistic. But because of that expectation, we undervalue whatever contribution Howard actually does make. (I am not referring to the person who does absolutely nothing, of course. That individual does need to be dealt with.)

# Parts Is Parts

There was once a television commercial that poked fun at a competitor who made chicken nuggets. The commercial claimed that the competitor threw anything and everything into the nuggets, with no regard for quality. The commercial portrayed a worker for the competitor proclaiming, "Parts is parts." Naturally the advertiser's nuggets were made of top-quality meats. The idea, of course, was that good nuggets must be assembled only from the best parts, and by analyzing these parts, you can tell if the whole thing will be good. We sometimes do this with teams.

As I explained in the Preface, this tendency to try to define systems by their parts comes from Newtonian physics, in which Newton's paradigm for the universe was that it was a big clockwork mechanism. That is, it was a machine. Based on this view, an understanding of the universe could be achieved by breaking it down into its component parts and understanding each of these. This approach is termed *reductionism*, and it has been our way of understanding complex things since the late 1600s, when Newton first proposed it.

To continue, once we understand a part, we have been taught that if we improve the performance of that part we will improve the entire machine. So we do this in organizations. We try to make the accounting department better. We fine-tune every aspect of this department and set up procedures for everyone (both within and without the department) to follow that will make it function as a lean, mean accounting machine.

You know what happens. The accounting department hums! But the burden is placed on people outside the accounting department to fill out endless forms, prepare countless reports, and so on and on. We have suboptimized the organization by tweaking the accounting department at the expense of everyone else.

Russell Ackoff (1978) has shown the fallacy of suboptimization through the following example. You decide to assemble a really fine automobile. You reason that if you can find the best components and combine them you will have a first-rate car. So you locate the world's best transmission, the best engine, drive train, axles, brakes, and so forth, and you combine them to make your car. Chances are that it will be a pretty poor car, however, because the components have not been *jointly* optimized so that they will work properly together.

We tend to compose teams in the same way. We try to find the best of the best for each member we need on the team. It doesn't always work. They may not *click* with each other. If we put together a flock of chickens, we won't have a winning football team. Neither will a gaggle of nerds be likely to win the Nobel prize in physics.

We also try to suboptimize a team. The team is having performance problems. We look around and notice that Howard seems to be the problem. If only Howard would perform, the team would be a lean, mean machine. But Howard is obstinate, unresponsive, incompetent, or whatever, and, by golly, Howard is dragging us all down. Something absolutely must be done about Howard! Either he has to get his act together or he's off the team!

## But Parts Is Related!

The problem is, a team is a system, and a system is defined by the *relationships* and *interactions* among its parts, not just by the parts themselves. You cannot understand the human body just by understanding the kidneys, and neither can you understand the performance of a team by understanding Howard alone. It might be that Howard is very talented, that he could do a superb job, but his relationship with another team member (or everyone on the team) is really

> A system is the sum total of the parts and their relationships to each other. Being dynamic, it is defined by the relationships among the parts more than by the parts alone.

bad. They don't see eye-to-eye about anything. They are always sniping at each other or trying to stab each other in the back. It's not Howard's ability that is the problem; it's his personality clash with another team member that is causing all the grief.

This leads to the obvious conclusion that if we are going to understand systems, we must understand the relationships that exist among the parts of the system. What are the interactions or processes that exist in the system (in our case, a team)? Behavior has meaning only in relationships. If a lone person stands on his head in a room and chants "OM," it will mean nothing to anyone else, because no one else knows about it. If he stands on his head in front of a class on project management and chants "OM," that is altogether different. Many of the students might leave. Doing the same thing in a yoga class, however, would probably be considered acceptable.

In the case of the project management class, the head-standing person would be entering into a relationship with others in the class that they would probably consider strange and might reject. A group studying yoga, however, would see the person's behavior as appropriate. What is different? The *context* in which the behavior occurs; that is, the context defines what relationships and behaviors are appropriate.

> Each of us is a different person in different places.
>
> —Margaret Wheatley

One example that illustrates this is that my lecturing behavior is acceptable so long as I am in the classroom, but if I continue to lecture my friends during dinner after the class, they will no doubt consider me an arrogant ass. In the classroom, our relationship is one of teacher and students. At dinner, it is different, so the same behavior is no longer acceptable.

# A Paradigm for Teams

So just what kind of paradigm or model is appropriate for a project team? What should an effective team look like? What kinds of relationships should the members have with each other, and what behaviors are appropriate for them? Finally, how do we achieve such a paradigm?

A team is typically defined as a group of people who work together to achieve a common goal or objective, who produce high-quality results, and who enjoy doing so. The two aspects of this definition that focus on relationships would be the *collaborative* nature of the group and the *enjoyment* of it. Needless to say, a team cannot succeed when its members refuse to cooperate with each other. Interestingly, we sometimes promote such behavior when we encourage team members to compete with each other. We forget that competition and cooperation are opposites. You cannot compete and cooperate at the same time. So even though we want everyone on a team to put his or her best foot forward, this must not take the form of destructive competition.

The second part of the team definition is that members enjoy working together. This suggests a relationship of camaraderie, friendship, and mutual liking and trust. We know that lack of trust is a major factor when teams fail. There are many reasons why members of a team may not trust each other, but suffice it to say that if trust is absent, the other conditions of cooperation and enjoyment are not likely to exist either.

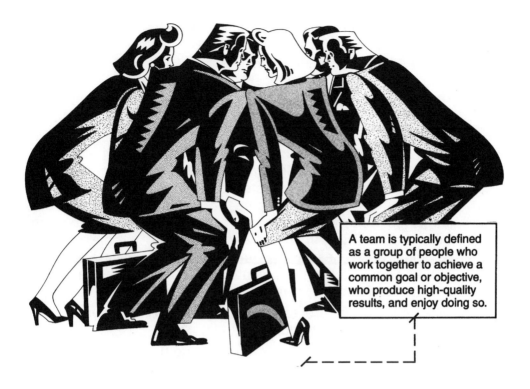

A team is typically defined as a group of people who work together to achieve a common goal or objective, who produce high-quality results, and enjoy doing so.

Other attributes of teams that we find when they are performing well include such features as open, honest communication; a willingness of members to listen to each other, even when opposing views are expressed; shared leadership; enthusiasm for the team and its work; a strong sense of purpose and of the importance of the team's goal; and a sense of interdependence. In critiquing issues, members attack the issue, not the person. They keep each other informed of problems, progress, and new data. They try to reach consensus when that is appropriate, rather than each person sticking stubbornly to his own position. They support each other in difficult times, and they show pride in being members of the team.

One way that you can better understand the characteristics of an ideal team is to think of teams you have been a part of and to describe the best and worst features of each. Then simply turn the worst features into rules that are positive and add these to the best features you have listed and you will have a pretty good understanding of what a good team should be like. You can do this in the following exercise by yourself or you can walk your team through it. It is a good team-development exercise in itself.

**Exercise: Creating a Vision of Your Team**

Do the following with your team, if possible.

1. Think of a team that you have been part of that was really great. Describe it to the other members of your team or, if doing this alone, write out your description.

2. What was different about this team, compared with others you have been on? Be specific. Was it something about communications? Was it the way members interacted with each other? Was it the team leader? Was it some *process* that the team used to get its job done? (Note that a process is any way in which something is done. This can include decision making, problem solving, communication, leadership, meeting management, reviewing project status, dealing with conflict, managing inadequate team member performance, consensus building, and so on.)

3. Make a list of the processes that will be involved in your team. How will you get things done?

4. Now ask yourselves, "How can we create the kind of team that we have just described?"

# SECTION THREE
# Team Development

# CHAPTER 7

# Turning a Group Into a True Team

The most neglected aspect of project management is probably the team-building process. We Americans, in particular, are so task-driven that we just want to "get on with it." Not only does this bias keep us from doing good project planning, but it also keeps us from doing any team building. Planning is seen as a waste of time, because it doesn't produce any*thing*, and team building is seen as a waste because it has no bottom-line relevance. It is just touchy-feely stuff.

Indeed, some of the programs billed as team building *are* just fluff, and expensive fluff at that. While people are involved in them, they get energized and come out of them on an emotional "high." The real issue, though, is whether these programs transfer back to the job, and in some cases they do not.

## The Need for Team Building

The best argument for team building is the sports team. While we may not always call it team building when a team practices, much of what is done on the practice field is definitely aimed at teaching the players to perform as a true team and not a bunch of "hot dog heroes." Is there bottom-line relevance to what they do? You bet! There is a

> **Principle:** Teams don't just happen—they must be *built!*

tremendous amount of money at stake for a professional team, and improving team performance is vital to the monetary success of the team. In fact, sports teams spend much more time together working on *Process* than they do on *Task*. The only time they really work on Task is when they play a game against a competitor. The rest of the time they are concerned with process issues. Furthermore, the attention to team building never ends. It is a constant, continuing activity.

# Can Americans Be Good Team Players?

I am often told that Americans are not good team players because we are *rugged individualists.* Because I believe in calling the shots as I see them, my response is, "That's a lot of nonsense." No doubt this country was founded by people who were rugged individualists, but that did not keep them from working in teams. How else do you build a log cabin or a barn, or cross the Mississippi when there is no bridge? How do you survive the desert and get to the other side of the Rocky Mountains? Not with an every-man-for-himself attitude. It required teamwork, and a lot of it!

No, I'm sorry, but that argument just won't fly. There are a number of other reasons why Americans are poor team players and, as a project manager, you need to understand them so that you can deal with them. The first factor is our educational system. From grade one through college, we are told that helping another student is cheating (especially on an exam). You are supposed to do your own work. Failing to do your own work is also a sign of weakness, and nobody wants to be a weakling. This idea appears to be changing, but it may be another generation before children from more enlightened schools reach the workplace.

> **Principle:** We have often been *taught not* to be team players. Helping others in school is sometimes considered cheating, and asking for help is seen as a sign of weakness.

Nowhere is this do-it-yourself tendency more evident than in engineers. Both as a former engineering manager and now as an instructor, I have seen engineers struggle with problems that another engineer could have told them how to solve in a heartbeat. But would they ask for help? No way! That would be accepting defeat. You have to work it out yourself.

Now I agree that we should generally solve our own problems. However, it is a question of cost-effectiveness. How long should a person keep trying to solve a problem that stumps her before she asks for help?

A study at Bell Labs found that networking was a major factor in the success of engineers (Kelley and Caplan, 1993). Those who were most successful used the informal network to their advantage. However, it was not just their willingness to call someone and ask for help that made the

difference. These engineers took the time to build alliances with other members of Bell Labs *before* they needed help. Then when they called another engineer, they got a timely response. Those engineers who had not spent time building such alliances would call, but their calls would often not be answered for days. The finding of this study was considered so important that Bell Labs developed a program to train their engineers to use the informal network and to build relationships.

Another factor that contributes to team difficulties is our competitive mind-set. As I have mentioned elsewhere, cooperation and competition are opposites. You can't cooperate and compete at the same time any more than you can be simultaneously happy and sad.

This mind-set (or paradigm) comes partly from having people tell us that the world is highly competitive, even cutthroat. It's a dog-eat-dog world, we're told, in which nice guys finish last. So when we are asked to cooperate in a team, this runs counter to everything we have been taught to do to survive in this world.

Another contributor to the competitive mind-set is that we view the rewards available to us as being fixed. The pie is only so big, I think, so if I don't get in there and get my slice, there won't be any left. This reasoning is even applied to intangible rewards like recognition. It may be true that there is only so much money to go around when raises are given, but there is no such thing as a fixed amount of recognition to be dispensed by a manager. Yet team members behave as if this were true, competing for the strokes given by their managers.

The interesting thing about competition is that it seems to be more powerful than cooperation. Countless studies of competition and cooperation have shown that if one party in an interaction decides to compete, the other side soon winds up competing, even though he might initially have been cooperative. So, once competition starts in a team, it can spread like wildfire unless it is stopped.

This does not mean that competition is bad. It just means that it undermines cooperation. So if you want people to be cooperative, you must limit the competition.

Finally, many of us don't make good team players simply because we don't know how. I have often said, why should I be able to make a living teaching adults how to work in teams? Why is this knowledge not taught in grade school, where it belongs?

## Learning the Art of Team Playing

Nevertheless, for those who have not been taught, we have to do it. There are several skills that are essential to being a good team member. These include listening, resolving conflict, problem solving, decision making, assertiveness, and openness. In fact, these skills need to be present before a team can function really well on the task assigned to it.

Often problem solving is difficult because team members don't listen to each other. We need to teach team members how to really listen to each other when they are discussing an issue. We all know that most of us don't really listen. We are too busy thinking about how to respond to what we *think* the other person just said.

> **Principle:** People need a number of skills to be good team members. You may have to provide training in these, since many of them will lack those skills.

One interesting outcome of this is to see two people arguing and to realize that they are both saying the same thing, but they don't know it because they aren't really listening to each other!

We also need to teach people how to plan, how to make decisions, how to reach consensus, and a host of other things, before they can be good team players. And we need to teach them, *especially*, to respect the ideas and opinions of other people. This is harder to do than it might seem.

As an example, I once did some training for a company whose management wanted to employ self-directed teams in their operation. The rule I follow is that behavioral skills should be taught first, then administrative and technical skills. So I was hired to do behavioral skills training.

I started with group process skills. After teaching them problem solving and consensus decision making, I had them work in small groups on some real problems. I was sitting on the sidelines sort of vegetating, when I noticed in one group that the team leader was summarizing what the group was going to do, and one of the women in the group was slowly shaking her head in a way that indicated clearly she did not agree with what he was saying. I waited for a couple of minutes to see if he would pick up on her nonverbal expression, and he didn't, so I intervened.

"You seem to disagree with what the group has decided," I said to the woman.

"That's right," she replied.

Then the group leader jumped in. "Doesn't matter," he said, "we already outvoted her."

I reminded him that they were supposed to be reaching consensus, not voting, and suggested that he might want to hear the woman's concerns before he accepted the group's solution. He reluctantly agreed, and they got into a heated discussion. Remarkably, at the end, the group adopted the woman's recommendation unanimously!

This is an important facet of group dynamics. Some team members don't have the skill to fully express themselves, or may not be assertive enough to speak up in the face of what they think is majority opinion to the contrary. We need to teach them how to be more assertive, and we need to teach team leaders how to be more aware of nonverbal communication that may signal disagreement.

Unfortunately, this can't be done in a three-hour session. I know all the pressures that exist today to keep people on the job, working. I am constantly asked if I can do my three-day project management seminar in a two-day format. The answer is no. Skill building takes practice, and practice takes time, and if you don't spend the neces-

> **Principle:** Acquiring skills requires practice. You don't learn to ride a bike by listening to a lecture.

sary time, you might as well not do it at all, because the result back on the job will be negligible. How much practice does it take to master golf? Or piano? Or riding a bike?

There are no doubt many other reasons why people don't make good team players, but I think these are the major ones, and the project manager must deal with all of them. This means that good teamwork might require training team members in areas outside their technical skills, and the project manager may have to take responsibility for having this training done because the functional managers of project team members may not do it.

It is most important, however, to recognize that you *must* do team building. Teams don't just happen!

# Use Project Management Practice as a Team-Building Device

It turns out that you don't have to do anything really esoteric to turn a project group into a team. Just practicing good project management technique goes a long way. The reason is that, if you follow the first rule of planning, which is that the people who have to do the work should participate in the planning process, then you get the following outcomes:

- Each member has a clear understanding of the team's mission and of the problem being solved and a vision of the final result.
- All members have had a hand in developing team strategy, analyzing risks, developing contingency plans, and then looking at implementation.
- During implementation planning, they have provided estimates of task durations, scheduled work sequencing, and had numerous discussions about the rationales for all activities.
- These group sessions help them get to know each other, learn what each person brings to the team, and value each other's viewpoints. And since they have collectively developed the project plan, you automatically tend to get buy-in to the final plan.

## The Project Locker Room Pep Talk

Since I have suggested that sports teams can help us understand team building, imagine the following scenario. A brand-new project team is meeting for the first time. The project manager is acting as the team's coach and is introducing members to the assignment they have been given. Further, let's assume that the project manager had very little choice in the people assigned to the team. The pep talk might sound like this:

*Okay, troops, you all know why you're here. We've been selected to develop a new Quadromatic Phasor Drive for the 1998 Electrostatic Discharge Unit. Each of you was assigned because of your qualifications for this job. I don't need to tell you how important it is to the Company. Sales have been down this past year, and we're counting on the new EDU (Electrostatic Discharge Unit) to correct that problem. Now you all know what you're supposed to do, so let's get out there and get with it!*

Not only is this pep talk extremely inadequate, but it is all that the team will ever get in the way of team building. The project manager is interested only in the task and takes for granted that team building is not necessary.

## Getting Started the Right Way

The pep talk I described above is an exaggerated example of how *not* to start a project. There are a number of obvious flaws, but here are some specific suggestions for how it should be done.

First of all, because of our strong task focus, we tend to want to start by describing what must be done, and we fail to attend to any of the team members' concerns about themselves and the group. Psychologist Will Schutz says that the first concerns of people in a new team are about *inclusion* (Schutz, 1966). They might ask (if prompted):

1. Who are the other members of the team?
2. Can I work with them? Will they accept me as an equal?
3. Do we collectively have the capability to do this job?

So what happens when the project manager fails even to introduce members to each other? These questions remain unanswered.

Does it matter?

Yes. Schutz says that failing to resolve the issues that arise at each stage of a team's development will cause the team to continue returning to those issues in an attempt to resolve them. When this happens, team leaders feel that the team seems to continually lose focus (which it does), but this is often perceived as a lack of commitment to the job rather than simply a normal psychological reaction.

> **Principle:** Help people to get to know each other before you become too immersed in task issues. Failing to do so will just cause them to keep returning to inclusion concerns.

For this reason, one of the first things a project leader should do is help members of a new team get to know each other. In fact, if you can possibly do so, the best approach is to kick off the initial project team meeting on safe ground, that is, away from the job site. One project manager kicked off his project with a backyard barbecue at his home. As people talked socially and milled around, getting to know each other, they also eventually got around to discussing the project. Soon they were involved in very animated conversations about the project. The project man-

ager later said that this backyard barbecue was one of the best things he did in the course of the job, because the long-term effects were so positive.

The following list summarizes the steps you should take to get a new team started:

### Steps in Building a New Team

1. Introduce members to each other.
2. Together, develop a mission statement for the team.
3. Develop specific goals and objectives that the team must achieve.
4. Develop a plan to achieve those goals.

We have discussed introducing team members to each other. The next step is for team members to develop a mission statement together. At first glance, this might seem to be a waste of time in that most project teams are given a mission to begin with. However, what you get is a better assurance of a *shared understanding* of the team's mission, without which some members might head in the wrong direction. In addition, as I have mentioned previously, this in itself is a good team-building activity.

Once you have your overall mission defined, you can think of specific goals and objectives that must be achieved in order to accomplish the mission. You need not list all of these, but some of the more important ones are worth identifying.

Finally, you need to develop a plan for how to achieve the project mission and objectives. Developing this plan together has the advantages of gaining commitment, achieving a *workable* plan, and also building the shared understanding that is so crucial. One of the ten major causes of project failure is that something significant is forgotten in the planning stage. Having the team plan the project together provides some insurance that this won't happen.

## Team Building Is an Ongoing Process

It would be nice if the preceding steps were all that were necessary to turn the group into a team and assure that they remained a team, but this is not the case. Team building is a continuing activity. Using our sports team analogy again, we find that players spend more of their time together working on trying to improve than they actually spend on what we would call task performance or work. They are only working on task when they play a game against a competitor. The rest of the time, during which they are practicing, they are working on *process*. This is a focus on the methods by which they play, and the objective is continuous improvement. A team that gets complacent because it is having a winning streak is likely to lose very soon. Similarly, project teams should have the same focus.

No project team can afford to spend more time on process than it does on task, of course, but we need to spend more time on process than most of us do. In many organizations you will find that absolutely no time is given to team development once a project starts. In many cases this is because the team is so crunched for resources that team members don't feel they can take the time for team development. In other cases, it is simply a lack of awareness of the need for team building.

In any case, time should be set aside for improving team performance.

The procedure for ongoing team improvement will be covered later, in Chapter 9.

# How to Create an Open, Collaborative Climate

If you really want your team to be able to discuss issues openly, without getting into personality squabbles, then you need to build an open, collaborative climate from the very beginning, and to do so you need to model openness yourself. One way to begin is to let people get to know each other, as described in the previous section, and then have the group develop a set of norms for acceptable group behavior. You will probably raise some concerns by doing this—especially from your task-driven members—so you will need to explain your rationale. I would suggest saying something like this:

**Project Manager:** I know we're all anxious to get to work, but I want to make sure that, once we begin working, we don't get bogged down because of procedural problems. How many of you have ever been on a team that just couldn't get anything done because people were always arguing or sniping at each other?

I am sure some of them will acknowledge that this has happened to them.

**PM:** Right. It happens a lot, and I don't want this team to have those problems. If we pay attention to *how* we're going to work together first, then when we get to task issues we shouldn't get bogged down with procedural issues. Does that sound okay?

You should get general agreement at this point.

**PM:** Fine. Then what I would like to begin with is to have us collectively develop a set of group norms. Here's how it works.

The procedure for doing this is in the exercise at the end of the chapter. I have found it extremely useful in helping a team function with a minimum of friction. Here is a sample of the kind of list usually developed by teams:

- Only one person talks at a time.
- Be on time for meetings.
- *Listen* to the person talking.
- No side discussions.
- Deal with issues, not personalities.
- Keep your commitments.

As a general rule, the list should contain no more than ten to twelve items, and it can be changed anytime the group decides it is necessary to do so.

# Gaining Commitment to Your Team

If you follow the practices outlined in the first part of this chapter, you will automatically go a long way toward building commitment to your team. And you absolutely must have commitment. You don't want people to just be involved. That's not enough. People can be said to be involved just by being in the room with you. But that does not make them committed.

So why do you care about commitment? Because a person who is committed to a project should be willing to say, "While I can't always guarantee that I will do exactly what I am supposed to do, I will do everything I can to keep my promises." That is the kind of performance you are looking for. Without it, people may not honor deadlines, may not complete assignments properly, and may not attend meetings regularly.

How, then, do you get people to be committed to your project, when they have a million other things to do besides work on your project? Some guidelines were offered in 1958 by James March and Herbert Simon in a book entitled *Organizations*. These are summarized in Figure 7-1.

The first rule says that members of a team must meet together frequently to see themselves as a team. I believe that this is a significant issue for some teams, especially those whose members are separated geographically. I will discuss this more in Chapter 10, but these so-called *virtual* teams often don't qualify as teams at all, because the members don't see themselves as a team. At the very least, they must meet together frequently to do so, and this is often so expensive that it is not done.

The second rule says that people will be more committed to a team when it is doing an important job. What message is sent to members of a

**Figure 7-1.** The March and Simon rules for developing commitment to an organization.

1. Interaction among members of the project team will stimulate identification of individuals with the program and its goals. Frequent meetings will help facilitate this objective.
2. Identification with project goals by team members will increase as the prestige of the program increases in the perception of contributors. Perceived prestige is a function of the current success status of the program, the status levels of the present contributors within the organization, and the internal visibility of or attention accorded the project within the organization.
3. Identification with project goals increases the more those goals are perceived as being shared by other team members. Project managers should attempt to convince team members of the worthiness of the goals of the program.
4. Identification with the program will increase to the extent that individual needs are satisfied. Project managers should attempt to select personnel whose achievement (and other) needs can be met through participation in the program.
5. The lower the amount of competition among members of the team, and the less individual rewards are perceived as being fixed in sum for all team members, the greater will be the identification of project members with the program. This means that when resolutions are sought for problems that have arisen in the program, the program manager should concentrate his or her attention on the solutions to problems and depersonalize these solutions as much as possible.

*Source: Organizations* (New York: Wiley, 1958).

project team when people are constantly being pulled off to work on higher-priority assignments? That their team is not important, of course. If this happens only a few times, the project manager may be able to reassure members that the project really *is* important, but after a while actions speak louder than words.

Shared goals are essential for good teamwork, the third rule says. If you have ever been assigned to a team one of whose members couldn't care less about what the team is doing, you know how demoralizing this can be. This is one time when I feel that it is imperative for a project manager to take a stand. If you can't get the person to buy into the goals of the team, then you need to get him off the team, because otherwise he will sabotage your best efforts and drag everyone down. I do not say this lightly or callously. I believe that "the good of the many outweighs the good of the one," to use the words from "Star Trek."

The fourth rule is common sense: If there is "nothing in it" for someone, why should that person be committed to the team? He or she must have some needs met through participation in the work. These needs might include learning, career development, the interest of the work itself, a sense of contributing to the organization, and so on. We sometimes make the mistake of assigning a person to a project simply because she is highly qualified for the job, even though for her there is no challenge in the assignment. She could do it blindfolded. In a situation like this, you might actually be better off with a less experienced person, for whom the job would be a great learning experience. That individual might make up for lack of experience by sheer enthusiasm.

Finally, the fifth rule says to keep competition *within* the team to a minimum. As I have said elsewhere, competition and cooperation are opposites. You can't compete and cooperate at the same time, and studies have shown that competition almost always takes precedence. Furthermore, competition tends to turn destructive over time. If it were just friendly competition, we might not have a problem, but when people begin back stabbing, sabotaging each other, and so on, then competition has become a serious problem.

Naturally, there will always be some competition, even within the best teams. For this reason, it is important that project managers monitor such rivalry and try to manage it so that it does not take on destructive forms.

### Exercise: Developing Team Norms

Because teams must have frequent meetings in order to function well, it is helpful to have norms that specify how people should behave during these meetings. One of the best ways to develop such norms is to describe the things that have happened in the absolutely *worst* meetings you have ever attended. Have one or two team members act as scribes, to record on flip chart pages a list of these worst characteristics. Brainstorm the list without evaluating at the moment.

Once the list is developed, you can select those that the team agrees represent the most important and then reverse them to create your norms. Your final list may contain ten to fifteen norms. Try to reach a consensus, in which all team members can say, "I can support that norm and apply it to myself as well." It is not necessary for members to completely agree with the norm so long as they can support it.

Once the list has been developed, have copies made, one on a flip chart page, so that it can be placed on the meeting room wall during future meetings. If someone violates a norm, call it to his or her attention. Do this in a humorous way. You might pass out cush balls, certificates for norm violation, demerits, or whatever. Demerits might be redeemed through positive contributions to the team.

Over time, you can expect the group to develop new norms and possibly discard some of the present ones. So long as the new norm passes the test of supportability, it is fine to adopt it.

# CHAPTER 8

# Leading the Project Team

It seems to be an unchangeable fact of life that project managers have a lot of responsibility but no authority. I say it is unchangeable because I don't see many organizations setting up hierarchically structured project groups so that the project manager "owns" the people on the team. When you have no authority over people, you have to get things done through the use of *influence*.

> **Principle:** When you have no authority, you must get things done through *influence*.

If you are ineffective as a leader, if you lack the respect and trust of team members, you will be unable to exercise influence.

## The Need for Leadership

Managing and leading are not the same. We have all known managers who were not leaders, and sometimes we meet leaders who are not good managers, although I don't think a person can be a good leader if he or she is totally incompetent as a manager because that would cost the person the respect of team members.

The word *manage* comes from the French and originally meant that the person handled horses. It still connotes handling things or doing administrative work. Thus a manager will be good at planning, organizing, controlling, and so on. To be a leader, on the other hand, means that you can get people to follow you wherever you go. In fact, one of the best definitions of leadership I have found was given by Vance Packard, as shown in the box.

> **Leadership:** the art of getting people to want to do something that you are convinced should be done.
>
> —Vance Packard

The key word in that definition is *want*. You can get people to do what you think should be done in a lot of ways: You can bribe, coerce, beg, pay, or shame them into doing it. But to get them to *want* to do it is the essence of leadership.

Now the real question is, how do you get someone to want to do something? This takes us back to the subject of motivation, which was discussed in Chapter 4. To get someone to want to do something means that you must have a sense of what that person's needs are, so you have to take some interest in your team members. In fact, I believe this is an essential ingredient of true leadership—you have to be concerned with and to care about your followers to be effective.

I once had a fellow say to me, "I understand that to be effective as a manager you're supposed to take a personal interest in the people that report to you. You're supposed to ask about the wife and kid and the family dog. Frankly, I don't care about that stuff. What should I do?"

I told him to forget about being a manager, because I didn't think he would be effective in that role. Furthermore, I don't believe that you can fake it when you don't really care, so I could not advise him to do that. To me, when someone fakes caring, it always comes across as shallow and manipulative, and I think people resent it. Ultimately, then, it backfires. (Incidentally, this guy agreed with me. He was only considering being a manager because his boss was pushing him in that direction, but he really preferred staying in a technical job.)

> **Principle:** A leader must achieve organizational results while helping employees achieve their career objectives.

I believe the key to leadership can be summed up by saying that a project leader is concerned with meeting project objectives while simultaneously helping members of the project team achieve their career objectives. As I explained in Chapter 4, the employment relation is an *exchange* agreement, and if it is not equitable for both parties it cannot work for long.

James L. Vincent, CEO of Biogen, Inc., has written that we need strong leaders today and suggests that they must have the following qualities:

- Strong values that allow him or her to be scrupulously, intellectually honest, able to admit being wrong, and to respond accordingly
- A willingness to take reasonable risks, with little fear of failure
- High energy, intensity, and focus—and the ability to inspire these qualities in others
- An ego strong enough to tolerate a lot of uncertainty, to surround

oneself with high-capacity people, and to ignite in them a can-do spirit (Vincent, 1996)

# The Practice of Phony Leadership

There have probably been more books written on leadership than on any other management subject. Perhaps this is because there are so few managers who are true leaders that the authors hope their books will make a difference. I think a significant reason for the lack of leadership was discovered by Stephen Covey, who described it in his best-selling book *The 7 Habits of Highly Effective People*. Covey writes:

> As my study took me back through [the past] 200 years of writing about success, I noticed a startling pattern emerging . . . it was filled with social image consciousness, techniques and quick fixes—with social band-aids and aspirin that addressed acute problems and sometimes even appeared to solve them temporarily, but left the underlying chronic problems untouched to fester and resurface time and again.
>
> In stark contrast, almost all the literature in the first 150 years or so focused on what could be called the *Character Ethic* as the foundation of success—things like integrity, humility, fidelity, temperance, courage, justice, patience, industry, simplicity, modesty, and the Golden Rule (Covey, 1990, p. 18).

As Covey goes on to say, much of the *Personality Ethic* literature is self-centered, manipulative, and deceptive. While some of it does acknowledge character as being important, by and large this is just lip service, with the primary thrust being on influence techniques, power strategies, communication skills, and positive attitudes. It encourages a "do unto them before they do unto you" outlook. Now translate this into management practice, and you will note that we have managers operating in the same vein. Peter Drucker acknowledged this in his book *Management: Tasks, Responsibilities, Practices* (1973) when he said that much of management practice is manipulative. I don't believe that manipulation can pass for leadership, because most manipulation is not based on the idea of a fair exchange but rather, on getting what the manipulator wants at the lowest possible cost to himself. In short, it generally means taking advantage of people.

We have seen an increasing disregard for people in corporate America over the past decade as exemplified by all the downsizing (sometimes called *rightsizing* or *reengineering*) that has occurred, much of which is

Manipulation cannot pass as leadership.

aimed only at fixing the bottom line for the benefit of stockholders and top executives in the corporation. The cost to this country in human suffering has been enormous, and the price we are likely to pay over the long run cannot be calculated, but rest assured, the price will be paid (see Downs, *Corporate Executions*, 1995, for a fuller treatment of this subject). Already it is causing problems for managers of teams, because of the fear and distrust engendered in employees who know they may be in the next cutback. This is discussed more fully in Chapter 13 as one of the barriers to team performance.

## The Practice of True Leadership

As Vance Packard's definition suggests, true leaders have the interests of employees in mind. But how do you *practice* leadership? What do you do that people call leadership? Clearly it is not a position, but a way of behaving.

> **Principle:** Leadership is not a position but a way of behaving.

There have been hundreds of academic studies on leadership, most of them designed to determine whether there are personality correlates with good leadership. The answer is a definitive *no*. The conclusion is that leadership is determined by what you *do*, not by some traits that you were born with or managed to acquire along the way. The good news is that almost anyone can learn behaviors and thereby exercise leadership, whereas if leadership ability depended on inborn traits, only a comparative few of us could ever be leaders.

One of the more recent studies of leadership was conducted by James Kouzes and Barry Posner (1988), and it confirmed the previous findings. In their study, Kouzes and Posner asked leaders throughout the United States to explain what they were doing when they were getting good results from their teams and companies. The researchers found that effective leaders engaged in five practices, which can be more fully described by two subpractices each. These are summarized in Figure 8-1.

The first practice, *challenging the process*, indicates that effective leaders do not fall into the trap of saying, "If it ain't broke, don't fix it." Instead, they are always searching for opportunities to make improvements. Also, since they know that you can't try new things without some risk, they are willing to experiment, with the understanding that some of their experiments will fail.

This practice in itself is discouraged by much of corporate America.

**Figure 8-1.** Kouzes and Posner's leadership practices.

*Challenging the process*
  1. Search for opportunities
  2. Experiment and take risks

*Inspiring a shared vision*
  3. Envision the future
  4. Enlist others

*Enabling others to act*
  5. Foster collaboration
  6. Strengthen others

*Modeling the way*
  7. Set the example
  8. Plan small wins

*Encouraging the heart*
   9. Recognize individual contributions
10. Celebrate accomplishments

*Source:* James Kouzes and Barry Posner, *The Leadership Challenge* (San Francisco: Jossey-Bass, 1987).

Many corporations are risk-averse, because they do not want to lose money on ventures that don't pay off. Marvin Patterson, formerly vice president of product development at Hewlett-Packard, has suggested that risk management should be based on expected value theory (Patterson, 1994). To illustrate the concept, expected value theory says that the expected value of a risky action is as follows:

$$EV = P \times \$$$

where $P$ = the probability of an outcome and
$\$$ = the monetary value of an outcome.

In other words, the expected value of an action is the probability of the outcome times the monetary value of the outcome.

For example, consider a situation in which a manager must choose between two options. In the first case, she can invest $100 with a 100 percent probability (certainty in this case) of a $150 return. (This might be done by investing $100 in a bond over a certain period.) The second option offers her a 50 percent probability of making $400 on that same $100 investment.

No doubt you can guess the option that most managers would take. They would invest the $100 in a sure thing. But expected value theory says that choice is wrong. Consider:

$$EV = 1 \times 150 = \$150 \text{ for the first option, and}$$
$$EV = .5 \times 400 = \$200 \text{ for the second option.}$$

Of course, expected value is based on the premise that if you were to invest a large number of times, you could expect the *average* return to be that given by the formula. But imagine a manager in a corporation who invests $100 in the second option (which would give a $200 return over the long term) and comes up empty-handed. There is a strong probability that in some companies she would be sacked or at best severely browbeaten for being foolhardy. Yet this manager could expect to show better returns on her investments over her total career than the manager who always played it safe. Because so many companies are risk-averse, I don't expect many of them to apply what Patterson has advocated in my lifetime.

The second Kouzes and Posner practice, *inspiring a shared vision*, is central to project management. Elsewhere I have said that a major purpose of project planning is to ensure that there is a shared vision and understanding in the team. In her book *Leadership and the New Science*, Margaret Wheatley writes:

> I . . . understand organizational vision as a field—a force of unseen connections that influences employees' behavior, rather than as an evocative message about some desired future state. Because of field theory, we can understand why vision is so necessary, so there must be new activities to strengthen its influence (Wheatley, 1994, p. 13).

Every project manager has to work with the team to ensure that the mission, vision, and objectives of the project are understood and shared by all team members, and when I say *shared*, I mean that the team has *bought into* the vision and objectives.

The third practice is *enabling others to act*. This, to me, is a very important practice, because much of what passes for management is aimed at just the opposite—that is, disabling people rather than enabling them. The reason for this is probably unconscious but can be explained through sys-

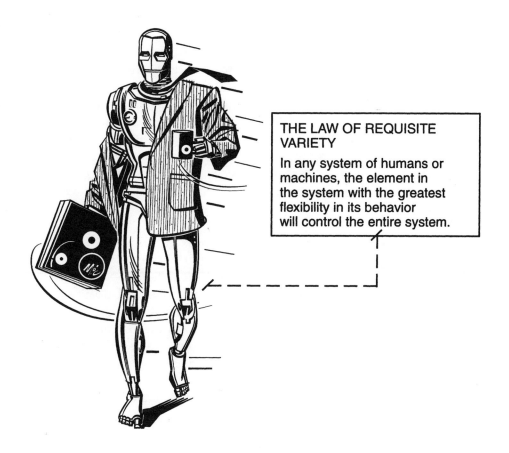

THE LAW OF REQUISITE VARIETY

In any system of humans or machines, the element in the system with the greatest flexibility in its behavior will control the entire system.

tems theory. As discussed in Chapter 4, there is a law in systems theory called the Law of Requisite Variety, which says that in any system of humans or machines, the element in the system with the greatest flexibility in its behavior will control the system.

The Law of Requisite Variety implies that a manager, who is supposed to be in control of a group (in the sense of seeing to it that they get desired results), must have greater flexibility in his behavior than that exhibited by the group. Consider what that means. If you have a group of six people, think of how many directions they can go in at once. The number is almost unlimited. So how do you achieve enough flexibility in your own behavior to match this nearly unlimited variability in the group's behavior? The answer is, you don't.

The only other alternative, then, is to somehow reduce the variability in the behavior of the group. The standard approach to this is to enact rules and regulations—I call them the "thou-shalt-nots" of the organization. Thus, we wind up practicing disabling people, rather than enabling them. Add to this authoritarian management, which essentially tells all employees not to do anything without being told, and you wind up with a group of zombies who can't think or take an initiative for themselves. Then we wonder why nobody goes beyond the call of duty.

Another issue that relates to enabling others is the need that many managers have for power. David McClelland (1975) has studied chief executives in particular and found that they have a very strong need for power. He further found that there are two ways in which this power motive is expressed. One is called the *personal power motive*. The manager driven by the need for personal power tends to be the dictatorial, do-it-my-way boss who stands for no insubordination. It's "my way or the highway," says such a manager.

Managers addicted to personal power talk in terms of "I want this done." They are concerned with achieving their objectives, and care little for the concerns of others. They have a hard time delegating, because they often have low levels of confidence that anyone else will do the job the way they want it done. They can be totally directive at best and tyrannical at worst. I remember seeing a *Fortune* Magazine issue that named the ten worst bosses in the United States, and, based on the descriptions, I concluded that most of them were probably motivated by the need for personal power.

The other expression of the power motive was called the *social power motive* by McClelland. Using this style, the leader says, "*We* can do this if we work together." Such leaders *strengthen* their followers, rather than putting them down. They inspire confidence and trust and are most likely to make people want to follow them. Based on his research, McClelland concluded that the social power motive is the one used by truly effective leaders. Those who use the personal power motive are generally less effective.

> **Principle:** Effective leaders employ the *social power* motive.

*Modeling the way* is the fourth practice identified by Kouzes and Posner. A good leader leads by example. She won't expect the troops to get their feet wet if she is unwilling to get her own feet wet. But most important, she works with people so that they experience *small wins*. She would never knowingly set them up for failure.

This may be one of the most important techniques for a manager to employ. I discovered it years ago when I started teaching kids to play guitar, during the folk music craze of the 1960s. When I started teaching, I looked around for instructional materials and made a discovery that had escaped me when I was learning to play myself. All the methods started by teaching chords in the key of C-major. The chords in this key are C, F, and G₇. Neither C nor G₇ present any major problems for a guitarist, but the F chord is very difficult to make at first. It requires strength in the left hand that a beginner seldom has. Not only that, but most parents don't want to buy a kid an expensive guitar until he proves he is going to stick with it. So they come in for lessons with derelict guitars that have strings about a quarter of an inch off the neck, which means that they need super-human strength to make that F chord. The result was that the student would come back the next week very discouraged. "I'm never going to learn that F chord," he would say.

I realized very quickly that this was no way to start, so I began teaching the key of A first, so that they had to make A, D, and E₇—all of them very easy. Sure enough, the next week they came back with smiles on their faces and confidence that they *might* just be able to play this six-string monster after all.

Planning small wins seems to me to be vital in getting a person or a team off to a good start. That's why I think team planning is so useful above and beyond its primary usefulness in getting the project done. It's actually a good team development exercise in itself. It's something every-one can do—given adequate support from the project manager—and members gain a sense of accomplishment from doing it.

I would also point out that there can be a flaw in the Pareto principle, when it is applied to problem-solving teams. The Pareto principle is essen-tially what we call the 80/20 rule. It says that 80 percent of your problems will come from 20 percent of your causes. Teams are encouraged to apply this idea by tackling the really big problems first; then they can move on to the easier ones. From a *small wins* point of view, this is wrong. It would be better to work on some easy tasks first, then move on to the bigger ones.

Finally, *encouraging the heart* is the fifth practice. The subpractices are that a good leader must recognize individual contributions and celebrate accomplishments. Again, note that this practice is in opposition to much of what takes place in some corporations. I have known too many manag-ers who consistently point out the sins of their followers but hardly ever give them a pat on the back. Actually, I think many of us are socialized this way. We are more comfortable trashing people than complimenting them. This may be more true of men than of women. Men often find it hard to pay compliments, but easy to criticize. The *tender* behaviors are for women, says society, and the macho ones for men. This is expressed as *Real men don't eat quiche and real women don't pump gas.*

If you would like to see a living example of the Kouzes and Posner practices, watch the movie *Stand and Deliver*. This is a true story of math teacher Jaime Escalante, who taught at Garfield High School in Los

Angeles for a number of years. He employs very unorthodox teaching methods, but has been extremely successful in getting his students interested in math. In 1988, eighty-eight of his students passed the Advanced Placement Calculus portion of the Scholastic Aptitude Test (SAT) and in 1989 the number rose to 109. Only about 2 percent of our students nationwide pass the Advanced Placement test, so Escalante is clearly doing something right.

When I saw the film the first time, I realized that he was practicing the Kouzes and Posner model, among other things. Unfortunately, because his teaching methods violate standard paradigms of how students *should* be taught, he has caught a lot of flack, and has now left Garfield High School.

## Situational Leadership

We have all heard people talk about the need to delegate or to be more participative, as opposed to being autocratic. These are usually thought of as various styles of dealing with people. The question is, when is it appropriate to use which styles, and how many are there?

This question was answered by Paul Hersey and Kenneth Blanchard in 1972, when they developed a model called situational leadership. This, together with the practices outlined by Kouzes and Posner, will give you a good set of guidelines on how to manage people effectively.

Hersey and Blanchard based their model on the findings of all that leadership research that I mentioned at the beginning of this chapter. The studies showed that if you look at the behavior of a leader toward a follower, there are two major dimensions that describe that behavior. These are called *Task* and *Relationship*. Task behavior is the emphasis the leader places on the work itself—what must be done, by when, and how. Relationship behavior is the support for the follower expressed by the leader, his willingness to listen to the follower's ideas, and the concern he has for the well-being of that person.

If you consider that these behaviors can be expressed strongly or weakly, then you have four combinations of them, as shown in the table, and each of these four has been given a name to designate the different styles of leadership. The table also shows when it is appropriate to use each style.

The appropriate style depends on the job maturity of the follower, which is determined by the answers to two questions: (1) Can the person do the job? and (2) Will she take responsibility for it? The answers of course depend on the assignment being given the person. For that reason, the appropriate leadership style will depend on the *situation*.

As the table shows, the answers you give to the two questions then determine the style appropriate for that task-person combination.

| Combination | Style Name | Appropriate For Follower Who |
|---|---|---|
| High Task, Low Relationship | Directive, Telling, Hand-holding | Is unable and unwilling to perform the assigned task |
| High Task, High Relationship | Persuasion, Influence, Selling | Is unable but willing to do the job |
| Low Task, High Relationship | Participative | Is able but unwilling or a bit insecure |
| Low Task, Low Relationship | Delegative | Is both able and willing to do the task |

It is important to note that situational leadership is a *behavioral* model. It prescribes how a leader should actually deal with a follower in a given situation. There are other models, such as Robert Blake and Jane Mouton's Managerial Grid (Blake and Mouton, 1964) that argue that there is a single best style of leadership, but the Grid™ model is an *attitudinal* model and suggests that the leader should have a high concern for getting the job (Task) done as well as a high concern for maintaining good relationships with followers. The two models are actually complementary, not contradictory. However, I feel that the behavioral model (situational leadership) provides better guidance on how a leader should actually deal with followers on a day-to-day basis, and that is what practitioners need.

> **Principle:** The best behavioral style of leadership depends on the person's ability and willingness to do the job.

Note also that although we have been discussing how to deal with individual followers, the same rules apply to the group as a whole. If you ask, "Can the group do the job?" and "Will they take responsibility?" you can apply the answer to find the style appropriate for the group, based on its present job maturity level. This will be covered in more detail in Chapter 9, on managing team development.

You can purchase instruments to measure your preference among situational leadership styles and the Kouzes and Posner practices from Pfeiffer. Call 800-274-4434 for a catalog. You can also visit Pfeiffer on line at http://www.pfeiffer.com

# CHAPTER 9

# Managing
# Team
# Development

No team comes into being fully developed, any more than people are born with fully adult capacities. Project *groups* must be turned into project *teams*. This is the forgotten side of project management, as I have said elsewhere. The project manager must develop his team. This is what most people call team *building*. To turn a group into a team, you must deal effectively with the team at each stage in its development. As is also true in bringing up children, failure to manage the team correctly in its early developmental stages may result in its never reaching full maturity.

Once the team-building process has been started, you have to manage it properly in each stage of its development. This chapter extends the leadership model of Hersey and Blanchard to team development.

The most popular model of team development, developed by Bruce Tuckman (1965), specifies four stages:

1. Forming
2. Storming
3. Norming
4. Performing

Each of these stages is characterized by different concerns or themes. The following table summarizes these.

| Stage | Theme | Task Outcome | Relationship Outcome |
|-------|-------|--------------|----------------------|
| Forming | Awareness | Commitment | Acceptance |
| Storming | Conflict | Clarification | Belonging |
| Norming | Cooperation | Involvement | Support |
| Performing | Productivity | Achievement | Pride |

*Source:* Adapted from Chuck Kormanski and Andrew Mozenter, "A New Model of Team Building: A Technology for Today and Tomorrow." In J. S. Pfeiffer, Editor. *The 1987 Annual: Developing Human Resources.* (San Diego: University Association, 1987).

# Managing the Forming Stage

In the Forming stage, individuals are curious about a number of issues: Who else is on the team? Will I be able to work with them? Will we get along? Will I be accepted as a full-fledged member of the team? What are we here to do? Will I be able to do my part? Is this something I want to be a part of? Notice that many of these concerns have to do with what Will Schutz calls *inclusion* issues (Schutz, 1966).

People want to know how they will fit into the team. This may be especially true in cross-functional projects, in which members are drawn from a number of functional groups. They feel "safe" back home in their groups, but in the project team, they are among strangers. Schutz has said that inclusion issues must always be resolved before the team can move on to the task. An attempt to bypass these concerns will cause members to keep coming back to their inclusion concerns, and you will feel that they are disorganized.

As project leader, you must help them get to know one another. This was covered in Chapter 7, where it was pointed out that is important to deal with what many consider a "soft" issue before tackling the "hard" ones. Help team members especially to find out what competencies each person brings to the team, and try to clarify for each of them what role they will play in the team. If possible, spend the first session together in a nonthreatening social setting, with no attempt to "get to work." Just let them get to know each other and outline for them the project's main objectives and explain how they fit in. Later you can begin planning the project with them.

As the forming stage progresses, you will have to give the team a lot of direction. This does not mean telling people how to do their jobs, especially if it is a cross-functional team, but it does mean direction in the sense of getting organized. Planning the project is one of the best team-building activities I know of. You don't need to take them to a ropes course (no harm done if you do, but it isn't necessary). Remember, a key purpose of project planning is to ensure that the members have a *shared understanding* of what the team is trying to do and how it will go about the work. Developing a mission statement together helps build that shared understanding and vision.

It is also helpful in this stage to go through values clarification and to develop a set of team norms. Procedures are presented in Chapters 5 and 7. Further, you must ensure that the roles of all team members are well defined and that working procedures are agreed upon. This includes your role as team leader. Sometimes people have unrealistic expectations of the team leader's role. For example, they think you should be a technical expert, which is not possible in a cross-functional team. Instead, you serve more as a resource to them. If they need help, you will get it for them. You will also represent them to senior management, particularly where misunderstandings or conflict might occur.

In particular, you must get all members committed to the team. A way of doing this was outlined in Chapter 7. This is undoubtedly harder with teams that are geographically dispersed than it is with those in which all members are at the same location. In fact, I even have a hard time calling such groups teams, and think the term *virtual team* is an oxymoron. The basic definition of a team is that its members *work together*, meaning collaboratively, to get the job done. In virtual teams they really work independently of each other, and this creates major problems for everyone.

## Coping With Virtual Teams

If you are running a virtual team like this, you must communicate frequently with the members at a distance. Daily conversations are best. This can wreck havoc with your personal life when there is an eight- to twelve-hour time difference between you. Of necessity, someone will have to talk during his personal time.

You will also find that videoconferencing has its problems. This approach is touted as solving the problem of being separated. But I have talked to a good sample of people who have used it, and they all report the same thing: You can't achieve the same effect with videoconferencing that you get face-to-face. You can't see the subtle nonverbal nuances on video that you can detect in person. Further, there really is limited *interaction* over video. Each person acts and the others react individually. That is not the effect that you get when the group is sitting around the same table.

I understand that such projects will be necessary for some teams, and videoconferencing is certainly better than no communication. Still, I recommend that you periodically get the team together for a face-to-face meeting, and this is especially important at the beginning of the project. My conviction is that you either pay now or you pay later, and it is always cheaper to pay now. So, while it is expensive to bring a group together when its members are spread all over the planet, it is less expensive than wasting huge sums on false starts and rework that are otherwise likely to occur. In this Forming stage, team members want the leader to help them get organized, to resolve differing points of view, and to help them define roles and responsibilities. Weak leadership at this point may make it impossible for you to be effective later on. As we saw in Chapter 8, the leadership style that is appropriate at this stage is called *Directive* by Hersey and Blanchard. This does not mean that you are a dictator, of course. You are there to facilitate getting plans made and to provide structure.

## How to Survive the Storming Stage

In the Storming stage, conflict breaks out. Members argue about the team's mission, goals, and objectives. Are we on the right track? Are you sure? Who is calling the shots, making decisions, and so on? Do I really want to continue as a member of this team? Is the leader really competent? Does she know what she's doing? In short, this is the stage in which your role as leader will often be challenged. The appropriate leadership role here is the Selling or Influence style described in Chapter 8. You must resolve conflicts, sell the team on the validity of the mission that has been given, and assure members that they are on the right track (or get them back on track if this is not true).

This is the most difficult stage to navigate—especially for project managers who do not like dealing with conflict. The tendency here is to rush through this stage as quickly as possible, often by pretending that the conflict does not exist. Wrong strategy!

The conflict does exist, and it won't go away simply by pretending that everyone loves everyone else. The conflict must be managed so that it does not become destructive, but if this does happen, the conflict must be resolved. How this is done is covered in

> **Principle:** Conflict won't go away by pretending it doesn't exist. It must be managed or resolved.

Chapter 16. The basic premise, though, is that conflict is not all bad. You need a conflict of ideas in order to have innovation in a team. We say that

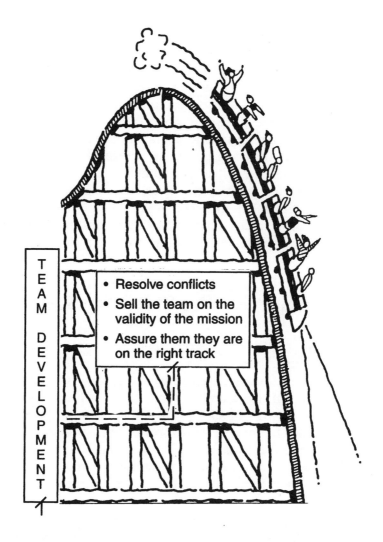

such conflict should be *managed*. You invite dissent, but at the same time teach people to critique ideas, not blast each other.

The really hard one for many managers is when the team starts attacking you as the leader. You aren't doing a good job, they say. Maybe someone else should manage the project. This can be very uncomfortable, but if you let them put you on the defensive and fall into the trap of arguing with them, you may lose it altogether.

When you are attacked, you might respond with, "So you feel that I'm not doing the job the way it should be done? Tell me why you feel that way."

This response will often defuse the person's hostility and make him more willing to discuss his concerns logically. It also goes a long way toward developing an open, collaborative climate, which is essential for generating innovative capacity.

You must allow team members time for a certain amount of venting when they are in the Storming stage, but eventually you will have to make it clear that they have a job to do and that they need to resolve their concerns and get on with the work. To the degree that you honor their fear, anger, and distrust, you will allow them to work through these feelings. If you suggest that they are not appropriate, then you simply alienate them.

## The Positive Role of Feelings

When I was just getting started in my career, it was common to hear managers say that you should leave your feelings outside when you came to work. This was in 1964. I always felt indignant about this, because it was clearly ridiculous. You can't walk into a building and leave your feelings outside. That's part of what makes us human. If you want to deal with robots, fine, but they don't have the creative capacity of humans, and some of that creativity comes from emotion.

What is really ironic is that these same managers wanted their employees to be motivated. Note that there is a common root for the words *emotion* and *motivate*. So what they were really saying was, "Leave your negative emotions outside and just bring in your positive ones." It was a long time before I realized why they wanted it that way: They didn't know how to deal with emotion.

We often avoid conflict because it gets unpleasant, and we also don't know how to handle it. A team member does something to irritate another member. That person says nothing to the irritating person, but complains to others. We used to talk about this in Transactional Analysis as *saving up brown stamps*. Then, when we had saved up enough of them, we *cashed them in*. What this means is that the resentment builds up to the breaking point, at which point the offended person trashes the other. The explosion seems completely out of line with the minor offense that was its immediate cause, and the irritating person is bewildered.

Sometimes the person responds by saying, "Why didn't you tell me that what I was doing bothered you?"

"You should have known better!" protests the brown stamp saver.

"I can't read your mind—if you even have one!" yells the stamp giver. Sound familiar?

We managers sometimes avoid confronting employee performance issues, because the person might get upset and, heaven help us, might even cry. That is devastating. About the worst thing that can happen to you as a manager is to make someone cry when you suggest that her performance is unsatisfactory. Rather than face that possibility, we try every other option we can find.

There's no denying that it is unpleasant. But it is also necessary, if you are going to get through the Storming stage, to deal with conflict, because if you don't the team will continue to experience it and may never get to the Norming stage and certainly won't reach performing. There is more about dealing with conflict in Chapter 16 and about managing marginal performance in Chapter 15.

# Norming Is Nice

Compared to the Storming stage, this one is Nirvana. By the time a team reaches the Norming stage, team members are beginning to cooperate with each other. They have "bought in" to the project and are very much involved in the work. Further, they have started to support each other. They now think of themselves as a team. Up to this point, they may have maintained a wait-and-see attitude. Before this stage is reached, if you had asked them if they wanted to choose a team name, buy jackets or hats, or some other indication that they were part of a team, they might have done so halfheartedly. In the Norming stage, their perception of themselves as a team is more fully developed. In addition, they generally have learned to trust the project leader as well as each other. (If they haven't, they may not reach this stage.)

The name of this stage suggests that members have developed some norms about how to work together. A norm is a generally agreed-upon "rule" of behavior. For example, the rule to "deal with issues, not personalities" is a norm. You can actually save team members some time by helping them develop a set of group norms while they are in the Forming stage, so that when they reach this stage, those norms tend to solidify.

In this stage you can adopt a Participative leadership style. You give group members more latitude in making decisions about how team issues should be handled. A Participative style involves less task emphasis on your part and more relationship behavior. Your relationship behavior should take the form of supporting members, let-

> **Principle:** You will never learn whether you can trust someone unless you are willing to take a risk.

ting them know you have confidence in them, and encouraging them to continue being cooperative with each other.

Participative management is hard for some managers. It requires that you trust people, and there is always risk involved in this. You are giving team members more freedom to "do their own thing," and the possibility is that someone might drop the ball and create problems for you. The thing is, you can't develop trust without taking a chance. That is, if you never let someone have free rein, you will never learn for sure whether you can trust him.

If you have ever experienced having a teenaged child get his or her driver's license, you will understand this. When she comes home with that shiny new license, you know what she wants to do—take the car for a solo run. At this point, there is only one thing you can do—give her the keys and sit down to pray and agonize. Otherwise, you will be hauling her around until she's forty, and that's no fun for either of you.

It is even worse with delegating, which is appropriate for the Performing stage. The only way out of the dilemma is to go back to the basic questions, "Can these people do the job and will they take responsibility for it?" When you reach the point where you can say, "I think so," you have to start letting go.

There is a real danger to you if you don't let go. So long as you are calling the shots, if anything goes wrong, the team can always say, "It isn't our fault. We were only following orders." So, if you want them to behave responsibly, you have to give them the responsibility.

# Finally—They're Performing!

The Performing stage is what every project manager wants to achieve. This really *is* Nirvana. Here the team is truly productive. Individually and collectively, team members are achieving good results. Cooperation is evident. Pride in belonging to the team is very strong. The team is now a *real* team, not just a group that everyone calls a team. At this stage, your job as project manager is fairly easy. Generally, you can *delegate* assignments to the team and expect that they will be carried out with a minimum of involvement on your part. Only occasionally will you need to intervene to give anyone guidance or even offer support. Essentially, they could do without you, insofar as day-to-day supervision is concerned.

This means that you can now concentrate on other things, such as looking ahead, conducting what-if analyses, and doing contingency planning. Like the parent of a mature offspring, you can "cut the apron strings."

# Suppose They Regress

No team will stay at the Performing stage throughout their life. There are two things that may cause team members to regress to an earlier stage. One is loss of a member and the other is increasing task difficulty.

When the composition of a team changes, its maturity level tends to drop. Any time a new member joins a team, either to replace someone else or because more people are needed at a new phase of the project, you must deal with inclusion concerns again. For goodness sake, help the new person get to know the others and them to know her as quickly as possible. Don't just toss this person into the fray and expect that the inclusion issues will automatically be resolved. They may, over time, but it always takes longer if you don't attend to them deliberately. Having been a team member in such a situation, and being an introverted person, I know that this is hard on the new person.

It can be especially hard if the new person is replacing someone who left and was well-liked; inevitably, the members of your team will compare the new person to their buddy, and almost no one ever measures up initially. This makes it difficult for the new person to get started on the right foot, and can even cause the person to fail eventually.

When task difficulty increases, the team may fall back to the Norming or even Storming stage. When this happens, you too must revert to the leadership style that is appropriate for that stage. Usually it won't take long to pull team members back to performing, so long as you adopt the right style. Continuing to be delegative when they are floundering, however, is sure to cause problems.

The leadership style appropriate for a team at each stage of its development is summarized as follows:

| Stage | Leadership Style |
|-------|------------------|
| Forming | Directive |
| Storming | Selling or Influence |
| Norming | Participative |
| Performing | Delegative |

### Exercise

1. Your team has reached the Norming stage, but one team member seems to be floundering. When you ask the questions ''Can he do the

job?'' and ''Will he take responsibility?'' the answers are a resounding ''No!'' What style of leadership do you use with the team? Do you use the same style with the individual who is floundering?

2. Your project is organized as a matrix. The problem person described in the first question comes from one of the functional groups. If he continues to flounder and jeopardizes your schedule, what should you do?

3. Consider your project team. In what ways have you arranged for members to experience small wins? If you have not done so, can you devise an approach for future implementation?

The answers to questions 1 and 2 are in Appendix A.

# SECTION FOUR

# Project Teams and Teamwork Issues

# CHAPTER 10

# Managing Decision Making in a Project Team

Until around 1980 there were a lot of people who strongly believed that team decisions should be made autonomously, that is, by the leader! When the suggestion was made that the group should make a decision, they would vocally declare that this was nonsense: "*Someone* has to decide," they said. They would use examples of the many bad decisions that had been made by teams as justification for their position. One of their favorite mantras was, "A camel is a horse designed by a committee." There are still probably some of those folks around, but there has been a broader recognition that autonomous decision-making can have its problems and is no guarantee of infallibility.

In fact, I think we might have swung too far in the other direction. As we have moved to having more team-based organizations, there are now people who think that you should make *all* decisions affecting a team by consensus. Naturally, consensus decision-making takes a lot more time than the autonomous approach, so if you insist that all team decisions be made by consensus, you have a hard time getting anything done.

The question that we must answer is: When should decisions be made by teams and when by individuals? That is the question that will be answered in this chapter. In addition, we will discuss how consensus decision-making—when it is appropriate—should be managed.

## The Nature of Decisions

Certainly there are times when consensus decision-making is valid and other times when autonomous decisions should be made. The question is, when do you do which? To answer this question, we need to understand the characteristics of decisions. Potentially, every decision must address two issues: One is the merits of the decision in some quantitative way. We will call this the *Merit* dimension.

> **Decision:** a choice made from among several alternatives.

The other is whether people affected by the decision will accept it. This will be called the *Acceptance* dimension. An effective decision is one that considers both dimensions when appropriate. This can be specified as:

$$ED = f(M, A)$$

or an Effective Decision is a function of Merit and Acceptance.

Of course, if you are making a decision that affects no one but yourself, then the Acceptance dimension is automatically covered, since, presumably, if you make the decision, you accept it. This is clearly not the case when other people are involved, such as in a team situation.

It is possible for a decision to involve both dimensions or only one of them. For example, if you are trying to choose a stock in which to invest, there is hardly any acceptance issue to deal with. The decision is almost entirely a Merit issue.

However, if you assume that several restaurants have equally good food (Merit), and you want to take a group out for a meal, and one restaurant is Thai, another Chinese, and a third American, there are likely to be Acceptance issues to deal with.

In practice, we find that both issues are involved in most decisions. A woman who likes both Thai and Chinese food may very well say that the two restaurants are not really equal in quality. The Thai restaurant, she says, has better food as a rule. Since she likes both Thai and Chinese food, Acceptance is not an issue, but Merit is.

Another factor that influences how decisions are made is time. If a decision must be made in a hurry, you generally can't afford long, drawn-out group consensus building. But you can't ignore the Acceptance issue either, so what do you do? You might, in the case of choosing a restaurant, ask who would object to each one, and the restaurant with the fewest objections would be the one you go to. It isn't perfect, but it might be the most satisfactory approach under the circumstances.

## Decision-Making Guidelines

One thing that should be clear to anyone is that Merit issues should be dealt with by someone who is qualified. If I know nothing about choosing

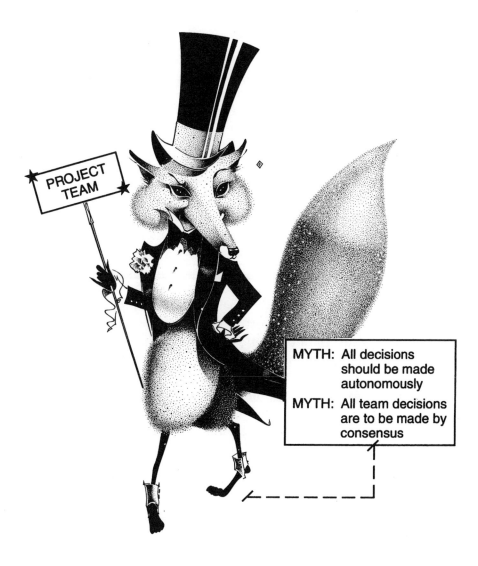

good stocks, I had better get some expert advice. That is what financial advisers are for. Similarly, let us suppose that I am a project manager on a job to design a nuclear reactor containment vessel. It turns out that a wide array of structural steels is available for use on such a job. The question is: Which one is best? In other words, it's a Merit issue.

The question concerns me, because a wrong choice could lead to disaster. How should this decision be made? Should I get the entire team to reach a consensus on it? Or should I make it myself, since the buck stops with me if there is a problem? Or should I delegate this choice to someone in the team who is an expert in the properties of structural materials?

The answer is obvious, isn't it? An expert should make the decision. Why involve the entire team when most of the members know nothing about materials? What will they add to it? Is there an Acceptance issue involved? Only in the sense that the members of the team are probably concerned that the decision be a valid one, and if they know it has been made by an expert (and possibly reviewed by another expert), they are likely to be satisfied with it.

Now consider again the case in which we are trying to decide where to have a meal, but let's suppose it is a dinner party, rather than just a luncheon. While there are merit issues, this is largely an Acceptance issue. The only way to maximize the probability that everyone will accept the final decision is if they all have had input. This means a consensus decision.

Finally, consider the situation in which both merit and acceptance issues exist, which may be the most typical case. Do we want group members to deal with expert issues that they know nothing about? Certainly not. In this case, we want an expert to deal with the merit question. She should help the group to understand some of the issues involved and let them have input on implementation concerns. This is called the *consultative* approach.

Consider this example. A family wants to buy a new car. The wife is a mechanical engineer, the husband is an artist, and the children are both boys, ages 15 and 17. Like their father, they tend to be artistic in temperament, and what is important to them is that the car be *classy!* Their mother, on the other hand, wants to buy a car that has mechanical integrity, good economic performance, and serviceability, and she is much less concerned with the appearance of the car than they are.

Using the consultative approach, Mom selects several cars that she judges to be about equal on the basis of her technical selection criteria, and the men can then choose the one they like best, according to their appearance criteria. Of course, if they hate all of Mom's selections, then some more negotiating may have to take place.

To summarize then, here are the rules for handling group decision-making:

| When the Issue Is: | The Decision Should Be: |
| --- | --- |
| M/A (largely merit) | made by an expert |
| A/M (largely acceptance) | made by group consensus |
| A & M (combination of both) | made by consultation |

## The Effect of Time on Decision Approaches

If a decision must be made in a very short time, you can't afford long, drawn-out group discussions. For the M/A situation, there is no problem, as this is an autonomous decision anyway. It is the A/M and A & M cases that are the problem. For those decisions that would normally be made by consensus (A/M), the group would have to use some time-reducing strategy. Maybe members will all agree to flip a coin or draw choices from a hat or just vote, with majority rule being accepted. The same may be true for consultation, or the expert may make the choice and inform the group of the reasons for that choice.

# What Is Consensus?

One dictionary that I consulted defines *consensus* as "general agreement or majority will." I don't like the majority will connotation, because a majority vote can lead to trouble when you need the full support of the group. On the other hand, consensus is sometimes taken to mean that the entire group agrees on an issue, when it doesn't. Naturally, total agreement is virtually impossible to achieve when the issues are tough. So why not just vote and rely on majority rule? After all, isn't that the democratic way?

It may be, but it has its drawbacks. In project teams, you want all members to support decisions that affect them, and voting often does not achieve this result. In fact, a school superintendent once said to me, "Now I understand why we always have problems. We regularly vote on important issues. Then I find, later in the school year, that some of my principals aren't supporting what was decided, and when I mention this, they say, 'Yes, but you remember, I didn't vote for it, either.'" Exactly! When they don't vote for it, they feel no obligation to support the decision. Worse yet, they may continue to actively fight it or look for opportunities to say, "I told you it was a dumb idea." Neither response is good for team camaraderie—or performance.

So if majority rule doesn't work, and it's impossible to get everyone to agree, then we're sunk, you say. Well, not necessarily. You just have to define consensus differently. What you want all team members to be able to say is, "While I don't entirely agree with the majority opinion, I hear you and understand your position. Furthermore, I think you've given me a fair hearing. And I can fully *support* the majority position." There is the key—the word *support*. If the person will support the majority position, that is often the best you can do.

Suppose, however, that you have a team member who says, "Not only can I not agree with you, but I certainly am not willing to support you. I think it's a dumb idea." If you need this person's support, you definitely have a problem. So what do you do?

There are four possibilities. One is to persuade the person that the majority position is correct. Another is to select another course of action that everyone can support. A third is to go the way the dissenter thinks is best. A fourth is to throw the person off the team. Each has a downside. Persuading the dissenter that the majority is correct may gain outward compliance without inner conviction. Or it may truly convince the person that the majority position is correct even when it is wrong. We have numerous examples of the majority being wrong. This scenario used to be popular in Western movies when a lynch mob was trying to hang an innocent person. Everyone watching the film knows that this unlucky fellow is innocent, of course, and the tension mounts as it seems inevitable that the mob will kill him. Then along comes the hero, who disperses the mob and cuts down the innocent person, just in the nick of time.

The second alternative is often a good one. Most of the problems that teams deal with have many possible solutions. If a choice can be made that everyone can live with, even though it is not the one preferred by the majority, then the situation is resolved in a way that gains the support of all team members. I know the argument might be made that since the majority solution is the optimum one, it would be mistaken to cave in and implement a less effective approach just because one person is against it. My answer is that you are better off with a less-than-optimum solution that can be made to work than with an optimum one that may never see the light of day. Clearly, there is no way to say that this is always the best

Kicking the dissenter off the team should only be done as a last resort.

approach. Every situation is different and must be handled in accordance with the total information you have.

The third option, which is to go the way of the dissenter, has merit when the dissenter is suggesting an approach that may be a paradigm shift. As was discussed in several previous chapters, any new paradigm is likely to seem strange to most people. So if the dissenter is presenting a new paradigm, it would be worth considering with an open mind.

Finally, kicking the dissenter off the team should be done only as a last resort. If you remove too many people from your team because they resist majority opinion, no one is going to want to be on that team. However, there are times when someone assigned to a project team simply doesn't fit. In that case, especially if his full support and contributions are vital to the success of the team, you may have no choice but to take him off the team. This is a soul-searching decision, and one that should never be taken lightly, but you must always "weigh the good of the many against the good of the one," to use the "Star Trek" saying.

## Avoiding False Consensus

Jerry Harvey, a professor at George Washington University, told a story years ago that has become a classic example of the false consensus effect (Harvey, 1988). He called this story the Abilene Paradox, and it goes like this.

A family in Texas is sitting around one Sunday with nothing to do. In an attempt to relieve their boredom, someone asks what they would all like to do. One of them suggests that they go to Abilene and have lunch at the cafeteria. Next thing you know, they all pile into an old car that has no air conditioning and are on their way to Abilene, which is 90 miles away. Now it doesn't take long to drive 90 miles

> **False consensus:** the belief that everyone agrees, although they don't. It happens when no one voices dissent.

in Texas, but the temperature is 100 degrees in the shade, so by the time they get there they are pretty grungy.

On top of that, the food at the cafeteria isn't as good as they remembered it and the sidewalks are rolled up, meaning that there is nothing to do in Abilene, so they are still bored. After walking around for a while and finding nothing of significance to interest them, they get back into the old car and drive the 90 miles home.

They get out of the car and are walking back to the house, when one of them says, "Boy, that was a real waste of time."

"Why, I thought you wanted to go," someone else says.

"No, I didn't want to go," says the protester. "I just went along because the rest of you wanted to go."

"Heck, I didn't want to go either," says a third person.

"Neither did I," says a fourth.

Then the hammer drops. "I didn't really want to go myself," says the person who made the suggestion in the first place. "It was just a thought."

So here they are, they have gone to Abilene when no one really wanted to. And why? Because they thought a consensus existed when it did not.

Now for the important point. Harvey says it is tempting to see this as a failure to manage agreement, but *it is really a failure to manage disagreement!* If they had asked if everyone really wanted to go, and if there had been a climate in which people felt free to say no, then they would not have gone to Abilene.

Note, however, that we often have group climates in which people do *not* feel free to express dissent. In some teams, a dissenter is called a *non-team player*, and is told "Don't *rock the boat*." Under such conditions, a person learns to be very tentative in his opinions, feeling out all the others to find out what they think before being willing to say what he really thinks. When everyone is playing the same game, it becomes very difficult to find out what anyone truly thinks.

## Avoiding Groupthink

Similar to false consensus is the phenomenon called *groupthink* as described by Irving Janis. This takes place when a group leader expresses a preference for a particular course of action and the group runs with it, regardless of its merits. Thomas Becket, archbishop of Canterbury, was assassinated in Canterbury Cathedral on December 29, 1170, because King Henry II had said, "Who will rid me of this meddlesome priest?" He later claimed that his remark was simply a complaint, an expression of frustration, but those who heard him took it as something he wanted carried out. This is a common pitfall for leaders. If they "think out loud," people are likely to take their expressions as something to be

> **Groupthink**: the adoption of a course of action or acceptance of a group leader's decision without questioning the merits.

done, and in King Henry's case a man lost his life. (See Follett, 1989, for an excellent fictional account of events surrounding Becket's assassination.)

Numerous examples of groupthink have been written about in modern times, such as Admiral Kimmel's suggestion to his staff that an intelligence report informing them that the Japanese were going to bomb Pearl Harbor was a smokescreen. By the time the bombs were falling, it was too late.

There is a standard way of dealing with groups that will reduce the probability of either false consensus or groupthink happening in a team. This procedure was originally recommended by Irving Janis and Leon Mann (Janis and Mann, 1977).

1. The leader should carefully avoid expressing a preference for any particular course of action in the initial stages of a group's discussion.

2. The group should be asked to offer options in a brainstorming fashion, that is, with no evaluation attached to the options during the idea-generation phase.

3. Once evaluation begins, *all* members should be encouraged to play the role of critical evaluator by looking at the potential risks and consequences of each option, no matter who offered it as a possibility. Such criticism as is offered should deal with issues, not personalities. That is, an idea should never be labeled "dumb" or anything else derogatory, because this comes across as an attack on the person who suggested it. Rather, the critic should say, "I have a concern with this option for this reason."

4. An attempt should be made to reach a consensus decision on the basis of the rule that everyone should be willing to support the majority position even if they don't totally agree with it.

5. If time permits, a final check should be made a day later so that people will have had time to "sleep on it." If concerns occur to them overnight, they should bring them back to the group to consider.

It is clear that this procedure takes a lot of time and thus should be reserved for critical issues only. It should not be used for routine decisions.

## Test Yourself

1. A group is planning to upgrade their computers. The big question is, what should the group buy? What type of decision is this?

2. A project team is trying to choose a new color paint for their office walls. Is this primarily a decision involving Merit or Acceptance?

3. Even though the team leader may keep quiet about her preferences in a decision-making situation, team members may still try to "pick up" on her choice. How are they likely to do this? Which step in the Janis and Mann procedure is designed to offset this tendency?

4. What is the false consensus effect?

5. Why is the Abilene Paradox situation said to be a failure to manage *disagreement*, not agreement?

The answers are in Appendix A.

# CHAPTER 11

# Promoting Innovation in the Team

In almost every organization today, the need for innovation is clear. Those organizations that offer the best array of innovative products and services have a competitive advantage over those that continue to offer the "same-old-same-old." In order for teams to be innovative, the climate in which they operate must support innovation, and some climates do just the opposite.

> **Innovation:** the act of introducing something new.

## Create an Innovative Climate

Corporate America is largely risk-averse. As I pointed out in Chapter 10, on decision making, managers who take risks that cost their companies money are often punished for their actions. Further, we push managers to deliver short-term profits—monthly or quarterly—when many truly innovative efforts require long-term investments before a payoff can be achieved, and this may adversely affect short-term profitability. As Kouses and Posner's leadership practices showed, good leaders encourage people to experiment, to try new things, and they are always challenging the status quo. However, even they will be retrained by a risk-averse climate.

One aspect of climate that can be particularly important is allowing (or even encouraging) people to have fun while doing their work. According to a handful of companies and specialized gurus known as humor consultants, corporate fun and games can motivate people, forge stronger bonds among employees, and relieve stress. The key is to inspire camaraderie and motivate, while stopping short of wasting time (Lancaster, 1996).

Does having fun improve the bottom line? Some studies have found that it does.

Another thing that affects innovation is whether people are willing to listen to new ideas. When people are closed-minded and cling tenaciously to old paradigms, then new ideas tend to be squashed as soon as they are presented.

## When Science Itself Is Closed-Minded

Surprisingly, such a climate often exists in the scientific community. We think of scientists as being open-minded, but this is only relatively true. Thomas Kuhn first described how hard it is for new scientific paradigms to be accepted (Kuhn, 1970), and Joel Barker (1992) has extended his findings to the nonscientific community. New ideas that violate long-held beliefs are initially rejected, even scorned. I recently saw a program on the Discovery Channel called "The Curse of the Cocaine Mummies," in which a forensic expert discovered that 3,000-year-old mummies from Egypt contained tobacco and cocaine. Where had these come from? Tobacco and cocaine are not known to have existed in Egypt. Tobacco was supposedly brought from newly discovered America to Egypt and Europe after Columbus's voyages. She conducted a thorough test to determine if the hair and skin samples could have been contaminated externally. The results were conclusive: The cocaine and tobacco were inside the samples.

Could there have been a trade link between Egypt and the Americas, she wondered? When she published her findings, she was ridiculed, and she said that some of the many letters she received from archaeologists were even threatening. Conventional wisdom was being challenged by her findings, and the scientific community was outraged. This happens fairly often. Michael Cremo and Richard Thompson (1994) have published a book detailing a host of anomalous findings that archaeologists reject. I am not suggesting that these anomalous findings are correct; I am simply pointing out how strong the reaction can be when conventional wisdom is challenged. It is almost as if it were an affront to sacred doctrine—and I suppose it is!

The medical community also resists new paradigms. Linus Pauling has been scoffed at for promoting large doses of vitamin C to prevent colds, and many of the claims of folk medicine that various herbs have curative properties have been rejected because the claims are not based on *sound scientific method*, that is, the use of double-blind trials, in which neither the researcher nor the patient knows whether a drug or a placebo (which usually is just a sugar pill or injection) is being administered. Medical doctors generally reject the experience of hundreds or thousands of years on the part of people who have taken a folk remedy and been successfully cured.

As Barker points out, scientists, doctors, and engineers are not the only people who can be "blinded" by their paradigms. All of us are subject to the same biases. Managers, for example, may cling to a cherished belief, even in the face of evidence that it is untrue. In the early days of the quality revolution that started in the United States around 1980, many manufacturers denied that they had quality problems. The auto industry, in particular, believed that Americans were buying Japanese cars because of price and fuel economy. It came as quite a shock to some of them to learn otherwise.

In fact, the quality movement itself has introduced a paradigm that is often unchallenged. That is the need for "continuous improvement." In its essence, the premise is correct—we must continuously improve our processes or our competitors will pass us. However, there comes a point at which a process should be eliminated rather than improved. Not only that, but the focus on continuous improvement can become a short-term one, and managers may completely overlook the need for taking long-term actions to grow their business.

## The Other Side of Blindness

There is, of course, a flip side to paradigm blindness. It is the tendency to glum on to every fad that comes along and to adopt it without critical evaluation. We have seen this with almost every new business intervention that has been developed. One of the most prominent is the team phenomenon, especially self-directed work teams (SDWTs). Unless an organization's culture is right for SDWTs, however, they should not be installed, so the first step is to survey the organization to find out if the culture will accept SDWTs. But there have been a number of cases in which a senior manager reads or hears that SDWTs have performed wonders for another company, decides that she must perform similar miracles in her company, and so orders that they be implemented immediately.

In one company that was trying to install SDWTs, I was told by employees, "We've tried every fad that's come down the pike during the last few years. We tried quality circles, and they didn't work. We tried employee involvement, and that didn't work. We tried stand-on-your-head and spit-for-distance, and that didn't work at all. Now we're on this self-directed work team kick, and it won't work either, and pretty soon management will be on another kick." The implication is, Why should we be committed to the latest fad when it is only the *program of the month?*

So the upshot of all this is that there must be openness to new ideas, but these should be subjected to critical evaluation (not paranoid rejection).

# The Intellectual Process

As I said previously, there is no doubt that we must strive continuously to improve our organizations, and this is true of project teams. The four objectives of a project are cost, performance, time, and scope, as was outlined in Chapter 2. Further, these are related as follows:

$$C = f(P, T, S)$$

which reads, "Cost is a function of Performance, Time, and Scope."

In many organizations today, people are being pressed to reduce the time they spend on tasks. This is especially true in product development. Target reductions in time are as much as 50 percent. That is, get it done in half the time.

Further, there is pressure to *simultaneously* reduce cost. At first glance, this seems contradictory because reductions in time are often achieved by applying more resources, which would raise costs. However, there are a couple of factors that permit both to be reduced at the same time. One is to reduce *rework* by doing the work right the first time. This will get the

job done faster and simultaneously for less cost. The other approach is to change the process by which the work is done. In product development, this process is largely intellectual, so what is meant is that you have to improve the intellectual process; in other words, you have to *think faster!*

Now you might argue that thinking speed can't be improved, but in a sense it can. Furthermore, some parts of the thinking process can be aided by computers. This was done in designing the 777 airplane at Boeing. Using three-dimensional computer modeling, engineers could tell before a model was built whether there was an interference between two components inside a wing. This greatly speeded up the design process (Sabbagh, 1996).

Now, before you dismiss the idea that the actual thought process can be improved, let me suggest that you study the literature on innovation or creative thinking. A number of works, by De Bono, Michalco, Von Oech, and others are listed in the References. I have applied these techniques individually and in groups with excellent results. In one case, a group of seven scientists worked for two hours to generate ideas to solve some problems that concerned them, and they developed so many ideas that the team leader (chief scientist) said it would probably take another year to work through all of them. He was elated by the outcome.

It is important to note that I am not referring here to the old group brainstorming approach that has been around for a long time. Brainstorming is just one of a family of approaches that groups can take. There are also a number of techniques that can be applied by individuals. Creativity is not necessarily better with groups than with individuals. In fact, very few really new inventions have ever been developed by groups. Invariably, they are the product of one person thinking alone.

The conclusion to draw from all this is that teams can benefit from receiving training in the methods of innovation because most people have not been exposed to these.

# Taking Advantage of the Organization's Informal Network

A study conducted at AT&T's Bell Labs was described by Kelley and Caplan (1993) in a *Harvard Business Review* article. The authors set out to discover why some engineers are so much more effective than others. A number of factors, such as being self-starters, emerged, but the most striking one was that the most effective engineers know how to use the informal network that exists within Bell Labs (see also Krackhardt and Hanson, 1993). If they have a technical problem that does not yield a solution after several attempts, they will call someone in the organization and ask for advice or suggestions. Less effective engineers sometimes do the same thing. However, there is a difference in the outcome. The more effective engineers receive answers quickly—the people they call will call them back—whereas the less effective engineers are often ignored or receive callbacks much later.

Why the difference? The authors found that the more effective engineers spent time *developing relationships* with other members of the organization, so that when they called, the other person knew who they were. The less effective individuals did not build relationships, so their calls sometimes went unanswered. Apparently the person they called thought, "Who the heck is he?" And, being busy, they sometimes ignored these mystery callers.

There are also some engineers who refuse to ask for help. They think it is a sign of weakness. So, when they have an intractable technical problem, they try to bull their way through it. I don't think there is any merit in struggling for a long time to solve a problem that someone else has solved, except that it might contribute to one's learning. From a business perspective, however, the cost of such learning is too dear.

Adding support for the need to build relationships, Margaret Wheatley (1994) writes:

> Power in organizations is the capacity generated by relationships. What gives power its charge, positive or negative, is the *quality* of relationships. Those who relate through coercion, or from a disregard for the other person, create negative energy. Those who are open to others and who see others in their fullness create positive energy. Love in organizations, then, is the most potent source of power we have available. This is because we inhabit a quantum universe that knows nothing of itself, independent of its relationships (p. 39, emphasis added).

You may think that this sounds very metaphysical or even that such ideas have no place in business, but quantum physics supports these ideas, and physics is one of the most exacting sciences we have. Furthermore, support for Wheatley's ideas comes from psychology as well. Relationships are the stuff out of which our organizations are built. In fact, Gregory Bateson (1980) has said that we should stop learning facts and focus instead on relationships as the basis of all definitions.

As a result of the findings in the Bell Labs research, AT&T developed a training program to teach engineers how to take advantage of the informal network. I believe that similar research results would likely be obtained in most organizations, so we should consider developing comparable programs for our teams.

## The Physical Environment Itself

Although it is outside the scope of this book to go into much detail on this, the working environment itself plays a part in making people more innovative. Some organizations have built special rooms in which groups can work to generate innovative ideas. These are usually brightly colored, they may have walls with Lego™ panels, and they usually have large white boards and a multitude of media, such as modeling clay, colored markers, and construction paper, that are available for use. Some innovation experts also say that a good way to start a group is to show cartoons for a few minutes, to get people laughing, because laughter is so important a part of the creative mind-set (Hall, 1995).

# Adapters and Innovators: Differences in Cognitive Style and Personality

Michael J. Kirton (1976) has studied the creative-thinking process and determined that there are two aspects to it, one called the *level* of the intellectual process and the other called the *style* of problem solving. Level has to do with one's intelligence, experience, and so on. Style, however, is a single dimension, anchored on one end by the innovators and on the other by the adapters.

Adapters, when confronted with a problem, tend to turn to conventional rules, practices, and the perceptions of the group to which they belong. This can be a working group, a cultural group, or a professional or occupational group. They then derive their ideas from the established procedures of this group. If there is no ready-made answer provided by a collection of conventional responses, the adapter will try to adapt or stretch a conventional response until it can be used to solve the problem. Thus, much of the behavior of adapters is in the category of improving existing methods, or "doing better" what is already done. This is a strategy that tends to dominate management thinking. It has been exemplified since 1980 by the continuous improvement process advocated by Dr. Deming. The flaw in continuous improvement is that you eventually reach a point at which a process should no longer be improved but rather eliminated.

Innovation is the characteristic behavior of individuals who, when they have a problem, try to reorganize or restructure the problem and to approach it in a new light. In doing so, they try to divorce themselves from preconceived notions about the nature of the problem and its solution. Their approach can be called "doing things differently," as opposed to "doing things better."

## Relationships Between Innovators and Adapters

Because of their different styles in solving problems, it is not surprising that innovators and adapters on the same team sometimes have conflicts. Adapters tend to see innovators as abrasive, insensitive, and disruptive. They are always wanting to change things, always creating havoc. Innovators see adapters as stuffy and unenterprising. They are hung up on systems, rules, and norms of behavior that seem restrictive and ineffective to the innovators. So, when the extreme innovator meets the extreme adapter, sparks are likely to fly.

## Organizational Climate and Innovation

As I have said earlier, the climate in an organization affects how much innovation is expressed. In general, organizations are inclined to encourage bureaucracy and adaption in order to minimize risk. This is especially true of large organizations. The aims of bureaucratic organizations are precision, reliability, and efficiency. Such organizations exert fairly constant pressure on managers to be methodical, prudent (this often means risk-averse), and disciplined. They are also expected to maintain a high degree of conformity. Note that these are qualities that are generally ascribed to the adapter personality. For a strong adapter, the longer an institutional practice has existed, the more he takes it for granted. So, when a problem arises, he does not consider changing the structure of the organization. Rather, he tries to find a solution within that structure.

The innovator, on the other hand, might challenge the existing structure and propose solutions that appear more risky and less sound to adapters. This makes the innovator seem less concerned with company needs as well as with the effect of his solutions on others.

What this means, of course, is that bureaucratic organizations tend to support adapters more than innovators, thus making incremental change the norm and making it hard to implement step-function or large-scale change. Innovators in such organizations often feel unappreciated, and may very well leave, thus moving the majority of the population in the direction of adaption and reducing its capacity for innovation. In a stable world, the stodgy bureaucracy can survive, but in a topsy-turvy, turbulent world, incremental change is often insufficient for survival. Yet the very person who might be able to save the stiff-necked bureaucracy from itself is likely to be resisted and resented.

# The Self-Organizing Nature of Information

As Dr. Wheatley writes in *Leadership and the New Science,* there are aspects of the universe that are chaotic and there are those that are self-organizing. One feature of the universe that has self-organizing characteristics is information. To thrive, an innovative climate needs lots of information, but it must also support those casual conversations that might normally be called time wasters. For example, I have heard that in the 1970s a handful of engineers at Hewlett-Packard were sitting around after working hours talking about the technical possibilities presented by the new semiconductor chips. One of their ideas was a tiny calculator that would have a great deal of power. A manager who heard them talking suggested that they start a project based on their ideas, and in this way the HP-35 and HP-45 calculators were born. Both were highly successful and spawned an entire generation of such products.

Researchers have found that this informal, watercooler aspect of many creative environments is essential for the conception of new ideas, the cross-fertilization of thinking, and the eventual generation of inventions. Yet, what you find in some organizations is that creative people are treated just like factory workers. They are not allowed time to have casual conversations, as these are seen as a waste of time, and a person with his feet up on his desk is clearly goofing off. But knowledge workers are paid to think, and some people think best with their feet up.

The emphasis on thinking even differs by culture. A fellow told me that he spent four years in Sweden, and sometimes in a group meeting, with the CEO present, there would be a long period of silence. To an American, such silence is unnerving. But the Swedes were thinking. The silence was spontaneous, and everyone understood what was going on.

He also said that on his first visit to a Swedish doctor, they started by introducing themselves; then he told the doctor his symptoms, after which the doctor sat down and said nothing for several minutes. This completely puzzled him, and finally he asked the doctor what was the problem. He thought perhaps he had some terrible disease and that the doctor was trying to decide how to tell him. But the doctor simply said, "I'm thinking." We are not used to that. An American doctor is ready with a diagnosis almost before you finish telling him your symptoms. This is a distinct difference between the two cultures.

## Software for Innovation

There have been a lot of techniques developed to help individuals and groups generate large numbers of ideas quickly. One of the best-known is Synectics, developed and taught by the Synectics Corporation. Now a software product has been developed that is based on principles from Synectics. It is called MindLink Problem Solver, and can be used by individuals or groups to solve problems.

In the problem-solving literature, we find that there are two kinds of problems—open-ended and close-ended. A close-ended problem has a single solution, whereas an open-ended one can be solved in many different ways. As an example, a math problem is close-ended. So is a troubleshooting problem: Once you find what is broken, you can repair it.

As you can imagine, most of the problems in this world are open-ended, yet most of our training is aimed at solving close-ended problems. The problem caused by this focus is that we want to frame all our problems as close-ended and apply the tools of close-ended problem solving. Unfortunately, those tools are not very effective for solving open-ended problems.

MindLink Problem Solver is used primarily to solve open-ended problems. These are called creative problems and cover a wide range of applications in organizations, including the following:

- Strategic planning
- Product development
- Market positioning
- Process reengineering

- Total quality management
- Human resources planning
- Training course development
- Personal career planning

The program works by serving as a personal or small group facilitator and helps spur people on to new and creative ideas. It is available for both Windows™ and Mac platforms. As of this writing, the Windows version is $299. Information can be obtained by calling 800-253-1844.

### Exercise

Get a copy of Michael Michalco's book *Thinker Toys* for each member of your project team. Have each member read a chapter to learn one of the techniques for innovation. Next time your group is working on problem solving, ask each person to describe the technique he or she has learned and then have the group apply it to the problem. Try a variety of techniques on each problem, since some will work better than others.

This approach makes it easy for people to learn by doing and, simultaneously you should get better solutions to your problems.

# CHAPTER 12

# Taking Your Meetings Out of the Doldrums

Millions of meetings are held in the United States every day, and, from what informal surveys of people reveal, most of them are unproductive.

| Efficient: doing things right. Effective: doing the right things. |

The way meetings are run constitutes one of the *process* concerns for project managers. Because meetings are necessary in the life of any project, it is important that they be both efficient and effective.

## Making Meetings Productive

When I worked at ITT, one of the managers there would walk past a conference room in which a meeting was being held and he would do a quick calculation. He counted the number of people present, then assumed some average labor rate for them, and multiplied the two figures. If ten people were involved and he estimated average burdened labor rates at $60 per hour, then the meeting was costing the company a minimum of $600 an hour (we are not accounting for lost opportunity costs). That figure alone sounds high, but consider that the cost per minute is $6. Thus, it is easy to see why wasting time in a meeting is so serious. And we all know that most meetings do waste a lot of time.

There is a video produced by comedian John Cleese entitled *Meetings, Bloody Meetings* that is a classic on managing meetings. In that film, the point is made that *the essence of good management is found in how meetings are run!* I had never thought of that, but it's true. If you can't run a meeting effectively, how can you manage a complicated business? We tend to lose focus (no clear mission), have no agenda (steps to get there) or timetable (schedule), and allow disruptive behavior to reign supreme. A good manager is one who can run a really effective meeting.

Catherine Dressler (1996) finds that some of the major complaints people have about meetings are that:

- Their purpose is unclear.
- Participants are unprepared.
- Key people are absent or late.
- The conversation veers off track.
- Participants don't discuss issues but instead dominate, argue, or take no part at all.
- Decisions made during the meeting are not followed up.

Sharon Lippincott, in her book *Meetings: Do's, Don'ts, and Donuts* (1994), provides five guidelines to help alleviate some of the most common problems. You should:

1. State in a couple of sentences exactly what you want your meeting to accomplish.

2. If you think a meeting is the best way to accomplish this, then distribute an agenda to participants at least two days in advance.
3. Set ground rules to maintain focus, respect, and order during the meeting.
4. Take responsibility for the meeting's outcome.
5. If your meeting isn't working, try other tools, such as brainstorming.

## Why Are You Having This Meeting?

There are four reasons to have a meeting:

1. To give information
2. To get information
3. To make a decision
4. To solve a problem

You might also include planning, but planning generally involves all four of the reasons listed, so there is no use in listing it separately. You might also have a meeting just to have fun, but that is generally not acceptable in business.

The point of this list is to help you decide ahead of time what you are trying to accomplish with your meeting—and, perhaps even more important, whether you need to have a meeting in the first place. Further, it tells you which people you need to have at the meeting. Be careful not to do too much, because this is what causes meetings to run on ad nauseam.

# Facilitating Meetings

There are a couple of major objectives that a meeting facilitator must accomplish:

1. Keep the meeting focused on the agenda so that the meeting objective can be achieved.
2. Get the most out of participants, which means drawing out nonparticipants and "toning down" overparticipators.

What follows are some suggestions for handling the more common problems. For an in-depth treatment of facilitating, see *The Skilled Facilitator* (1994) by Roger Schwarz.

## Handling Tangential Comments

There is a natural tendency for people to drift off the subject. Comments remind them of other issues that they think should be addressed. The topic under discussion at the moment is of little interest to them. Or they may just want to socialize. In any case, getting off track just wastes the time of everyone present and may prevent you from accomplishing your purpose in the allocated time.

If you are facilitating the meeting, your job is to keep it on track. When someone makes a comment that seems off the subject, it is best to respond by saying, "Can you help me see how what you are saying relates to our topic? I'm having difficulty making the connection."

If the comment is indeed relevant, the person can then explain the connection. If it is not, this is a way of making the person realize that it is tangential, and you can then request that she make a note of it so you can come back to it later, but gently insist that you want to stay with your topic until it is finished.

This approach is called the *relevance challenge* and is a way of handling what appear to be sidetracks without offending anyone. To just say, "I think that is a tangential comment" may be incorrect and is very likely to offend. Asking for clarification is more subtle and less likely to make anyone angry. Furthermore, after you have done this a few times, it sends a message to everyone that you are intent on keeping the meeting focused.

## Handling Overparticipators

The challenge to you as a facilitator is to get the most out of all your participants without losing any of them. There is a tendency for just a few people to do all the talking in a meeting and for some to say nothing at all. This may be because the quiet people have nothing to offer, but often it is because they are put off by the overparticipators. They may also lack the assertive skills or communication skills needed to fully express themselves.

I usually say something like, "I want to hear from some of the silent members of our group about this issue. Would those of you who have been making suggestions just cool it for a minute so the others can offer their comments?" Then I may specifically say, "Jean, we haven't heard from you. What do you think?"

In some groups that I work with regularly, we have developed such good camaraderie that I can I say to a member, "Willy, you've used up your quota. You can't say anything for the next three minutes." We all laugh and Willy sits staring at his watch for three minutes while the others talk. He also makes faces to indicate that he is about to burst, and we all have fun with his "difficulty."

One approach to getting more balanced participation is to go around the table and ask for a suggestion from each person. Group members are told that they can pass if they have no suggestions. This is called the *round-robin* technique and over the long term has the effect of establishing a climate in which everyone is expected to participate.

I should comment here that I don't think it is realistic to expect equal participation from all members of a group meeting. In fact, I feel that it is disrespectful to insist on equal participation and to force reticent members to speak when they feel uncomfortable doing so. That is why the round-robin approach permits people to pass if they have nothing to offer. However, I do have a problem with the person who attends the meetings and *never* contributes. When this happens, I deal with that individual privately and try to find out the reason for his silence and let him know that I expect *some* participation.

## Side Conversations

The best way to handle this problem is to have a group norm that prohibits them. When you do, if a side conversation starts, you can simply point to the norm (the list should always be posted) and the individuals involved should get the message. Or you can walk over right beside them, and that alone should be sufficient.

I have had a few people in meetings who don't take hints. No matter what you do, they insist on having their side conversations. In that case, I talk with the person off-line. Usually there is one individual who consistently instigates the conversations, and if you deal with her, the problem will be solved.

## Hidden Agendas

Meetings are often disrupted by individuals who are pushing hidden agendas. That is, someone is trying to accomplish something without letting anyone know what it is. I once sat through one of the worst meetings of my entire life. I was a consultant to a company and the president asked me to evaluate the project management process. He was having trouble with the manager of one of his departments, and he was convinced that this was a source of his problems. He called a meeting with his staff to review the points in the process where they believed problems were occurring, and then browbeat this one "problem" manager for nearly two hours. It was clear to me that his hidden agenda was to beat up the errant manager, and I was horrified that he would do it in front of his peers and myself. Interestingly, I could tell who the problem manager was the moment he entered the room. All of the staff looked cheerful except for this one fellow. His face had gloom and doom written all over it. He tried to defend himself when the president attacked him, but he got nowhere. Nothing he said had any validity with the president.

When I finally got the president outside, I told him that he should either work out his problems with this manager or fire him, because the relationship between them was so bad that it was poisoning the entire staff. He agreed.

The best way to deal with hidden agendas is to get them out into the open. If a person has a positive hidden agenda, and you can help him achieve it, then you are both better off, as the hidden agenda no longer disrupts the meetings. On the other hand, if a person has a destructive hidden agenda, then it would be best to talk with him off-line and see if you can get the issue resolved. The difficulty is that some individuals will deny their hidden agendas when you confront them, so the only thing you can do in that case is to insist on a change in their meeting behavior—if you have the clout to do so. If the person outranks you, then you might just have to grin and bear it.

## When the Boss Is the Problem

There are times when one's boss sits in on the meeting and is the cause of problems. There is no easy answer to this problem. The basic approach is to talk with your boss in private about his behavior in the meeting. Do NOT guess at his motives or accuse him of being "bad, mad, or crazy." Just describe his behavior, tell him what problem it causes, and ask if he would be willing to change. (See Chapter 15 for more suggestions on how to confront problems with other people.)

It may be that he or she is genuinely unaware that the behavior causes problems. Sometimes bosses are like parents, and take over the meeting you have called without realizing that they are doing it. They are so used to being in charge that they take charge of your meeting through force of habit.

At other times, the problem may be that you have a poor relationship with your boss in the first place. Maybe the boss doesn't fully trust you, or you have a different perspective on how things should be done. Again, you need to talk with your boss about the relationship and try to get it resolved, or else you may fall prey to the same kind of problem described above.

If you can't talk with your boss about your working relationship, then you have a serious problem that is likely to get worse over time. In that case, you might want to consider your career options.

## Dealing With Negative People

Occasionally we have someone in our meetings who is habitually negative. When the group is trying to solve a problem, these individuals counter every suggested solution with one or more reasons why the idea won't work. "We tried that back in 1909. Terrible flop!" Or "It won't work! The old man [meaning the chief executive] will never go for it."

Such individuals are terribly demoralizing to a group. There is a solution that I have used and have taught others and they have made it work. It is to validate the person's role.

"Wait," you say. "Have you gone mad? Validate his habitual whining and sniping? Never!!!"

"Well, hang on a minute. First of all, have you considered that public enemy number one (call him Clive) actually has a talent?"

"Heck no!"

"Well, he does. Clive is exceptionally good at spotting obstacles."

"That's for sure," you agree.

It's true. He is. It's just that the way he does it is disruptive. Now if we could just find a way to capture the *positive* aspects of Clive's behavior so that he doesn't cause problems.

Here's what you do. You sit down with Clive privately and tell him, "You know, Clive, you're very good at spotting obstacles that might keep solutions from working. The only thing is, when we're trying to come up with solutions, having obstacles pointed out too early in the game might kill an idea that ultimately is a good one."

Give him a moment to mull this over. Then continue.

"I have a suggestion. I want to make you the group's official *devil's advocate*. In case you aren't familiar with the term, it was developed by the Catholic Church. When a point of theology was being debated, someone would argue the devil's position so that all points of view could be covered."

Clive should be engrossed by now.

"What I would like you to do," I go on, "is write down all your concerns as we discuss various ideas. However, I don't want you to voice any of them until I tell you to. That way, we won't slow down the discussion. Then, when we're ready, I'll have you read your concerns, and then we'll decide what to do about them. Could you agree to do that?"

If he agrees, you tell the group about Clive's new role. If he loses his cool during the discussion and tries to express a concern, you remind him to just write it down. Then, when productive idea generation has dried up, you call on Clive to read his list. When he has finished, thank him, then say to the group, "Clive has expressed a number of very good concerns. Now what do we do about them?"

The net result of this is that you get control of Clive's behavior in a positive way, and you validate it for him and for the group. Clive is no longer disruptive because he now expresses his concerns only when called on to do so.

In one group that tried this, the naysayer suddenly became a valued member of the group. People started going to her outside the meetings and saying, "I have an idea I'd like to bounce off you." They now welcomed her comments, because they realized that you must identify obstacles if you are going to be fully successful in implementing any solution.

## Process Reviews

You can improve your meetings by conducting process reviews at the end of each meeting in the same way you do for projects. It only takes five minutes to ask, "What did we do well?" and "What do we need to improve?" If you make this a normal agenda item, people soon become habituated to it. At some point, of course, you will run out of improvement ideas, after which you can review process on a less frequent basis.

## Suggestions for Meetings

Two videos are exceptional in showing how good meetings should be managed. One is *Meetings, Bloody Meetings* by John Cleese, which is distributed in the United States by Video Arts, reachable at 800-553-0091. Another good video is *Mining Group Gold* from CRM Films. It was developed at Xerox and is highly effective. The CRM number is 800-421-0833. Rent or buy either of these and show it to your group, then follow the model presented.

# Improving Yourself and Your Team

# CHAPTER 13

# How to Improve Team Performance

One of my favorite sayings from psychology is, "If you always do what you've always done, you'll always get what you always got." That applies not only to individuals but to teams as well. Dr. Deming, the quality guru, used to say that there are two kinds of organizations—those that are getting better and those that are dying. And those that are standing still are dying; they just don't know it yet.

> Process issues always interfere with task performance.
> —Marvin Weisbord

## The Need for Improvement

It is very true in today's hurry-up-and-get-there world that if you are standing still, everyone is going to pass you by. Or, as Tom Peters puts it in *Liberation Management* (1992), the message today is, "Get fast or go broke."

Ten years ago the standard development time, from concept to first production, for a new automobile was about six to eight years. Then our friends in Japan got the development cycle down to around three years. That gave us quite a shock. You can't take twice as long as your competitor does to develop a new product. If you do, the competition can bring out two new models in the time it takes you to develop just one, and by the time yours hits the market it will be obsolete.

So we were forced to shorten our own development cycle to three years.

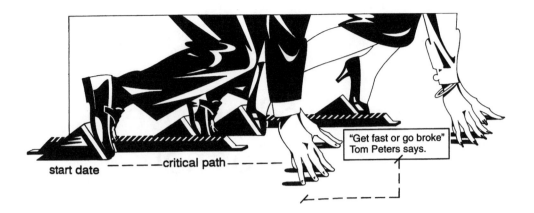

The auto experts believe it is possible to get the cycle down to a year. They don't know how yet, but they think it can be done.

One thing is certain. Most of the people I talk to in my travels tell me that they are being pressured to get projects done in half the time they used to take and, *simultaneously*, to reduce development costs by half, while maintaining scope and quality at their original levels!

Now that sounds totally contradictory. Generally speaking, if you want to do a job faster, it costs more money, not less. So how do you cut both at the same time? Well, you sure won't do it with the same processes you have been using. You have to find a new approach.

> **Principle:** If you always do what you've always done, you'll always get what you've always gotten.

Interestingly, when it comes to developing new products (this includes software, hardware, and even services), much of the process is mental. Thus, the conclusion is that if we want to develop products faster, we have to speed up our thinking, as I pointed out in the previous chapter.

And, as I have mentioned elsewhere, when Boeing developed the new 777 airplane, the company employed three-dimensional computer modeling to ensure that parts would fit properly, without running into each other (Sabbagh, 1996). Ordinarily, you don't find out these things until you build a prototype. Correcting such interferences can be extremely expensive. With computer modeling, Boeing was able to eliminate such problems.

The chief engineer at Boeing has been quoted as saying that as much as 30 percent of the cost of developing a new plane is rework (Dimancescu, 1992). He makes this point in a most cogent way by saying that this is equivalent to allocating one of every three engineers on the project to just redo what the other two engineers did wrong! If the rework can be reduced to 0 percent, that is a gain in productivity of the same amount. On a $5-billion project, that's a lot of shekels!

# Team Processes

In Chapter 11, we defined process as the way something is done. In the following list are some of the various processes that project teams are involved in. (You might want to add to the list.)

### *Team Processes*

| | |
|---|---|
| Leadership | Communication |
| Decision making | Problem solving |
| Meetings | Conflict resolution |
| Creativity | Designing product |
| Tracking progress | Planning |
| Risk management | Quality control |
| Customer contact | Defining problems |
| Change control | Record keeping |

All of these are subject to improvement. A common theme of process improvement is to remove any non-value-added steps from the sequence. Rework is an example of this. Rework is a total waste of resources. As Phil Crosby used to emphasize in his quality programs, "It is always cheaper to do it right the first time than to have to do it over" (internal policy of ITT Telecommunications).

In improving team processes, you may not need to do anything as elaborate as what is done in reengineering projects, but you certainly can employ the methods used by sports teams or the military. After every game a sports team tries to review its performance and make improvements or corrections. They do this in many cases by reviewing game films. Naturally, in projects you don't often record a team on film, but you can stop work periodically to review what has been done.

There is no entirely satisfactory word for this. We often call them audits or postmortems. Both words have negative connotations. We think of an audit as something done to try and catch someone in a violation or bad practice. Essentially, audits have a policing aura, and such activities arouse defensiveness on the part of the people being audited. The same is true if you call it a postmortem. It sounds like the project died. Perhaps the only nonthreatening term might be simply *Process Review*. In fact, we should consider the kinds of project reviews that are commonly conducted and be sure to differentiate among them. The following table summarizes the differences.

| *Type of Review* | *Purpose* |
|---|---|
| Progress review | To determine the status of the project with regard to Schedule, Budget, Scope, and Performance (quality) |
| Design review (applies only to hardware, software, or service designs) | Ascertain the status of a product being designed. Does it perform according to specifications? Will it meet target selling price? Will it meet customer requirements? Will it be manufacturable? |
| Process review | Solely to determine if any processes can be improved. Should *never* be conducted in blame-and-punishment mode. |

Process reviews should always have a dual focus. This can be expressed in the form of the questions that should be asked:

1. What are we doing really well? (We want to continue this, of course.)
2. What would we like to improve?

Figure 13-1 is a form that can be used to conduct a process review. If the form does not provide enough room, then simply use it to identify all the questions that should be asked.

> **Principle:** The most dangerous place a team can be is successful. There is always room for improvement.

Notice that we don't ask what is being done badly. It may be that *nothing* is being done badly. But the best team in the world can always find ways to improve. In fact, the most dangerous place a team can be is successful, because they tend to get complacent or arrogant. Team members decide that they can't do anything wrong, that no one can "beat" them, and the next thing you know, they're in trouble.

I would like to point out a serious pitfall in process improvement. It

**Figure 13-1.** Sample project process review form.

# Project Process Review

Project:

Prepared by:          Date:

For the period from         to:

**Evaluate the following objectives:**
Performance was on target □, below target □, above target □
Budget was on target □, overspent □, underspent □
Schedule was on target □, behind □, ahead □

**Overall, was the project a success?** Yes □ No □

If not, what factors contributed to a negative evaluation?

What was done really well?

What could have been done better?

What recommendations would you make for future project application?

What would you do differently if you could do it over?

What have you learned that can be applied to future projects?

makes no sense to improve a process that should be eliminated altogether! Unfortunately, the quality movement that started around 1980 has spawned a generation of managers whose primary focus is on improving existing processes, without ever questioning whether the process is valid. So that question should always be raised.

> **Principle:** It makes no sense to improve a process that should be eliminated altogether!

Also note that process improvement is analogous to technology advances. These proceed along S-curves, as shown in Figure 13-2. Initially, when a technology is invented, progress is a bit slow. Then breakthroughs begin to occur and progress becomes rapid. Finally, we reach a point of diminishing returns, where gains in performance are slow and costly. At this point, we need to invent a totally new technology. This same effect can be seen in process improvement.

## Conducting the Process Review

The way in which a project process review is conducted is very important. As I have already said, it should never be done in the blame-and-punish-

**Figure 13-2.** S-curves showing the progress of technology advances.

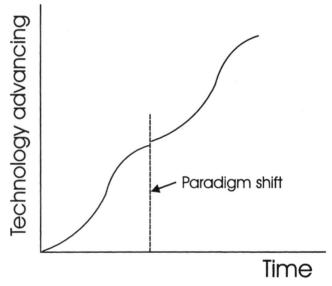

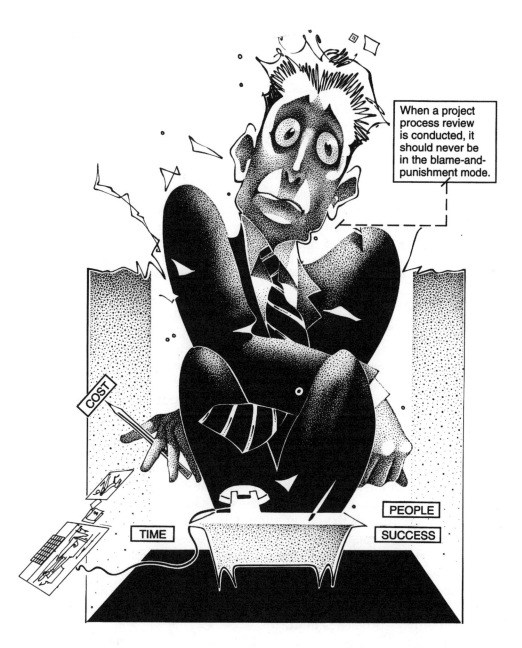

ment mode. If you go on a witch hunt, you are sure to find a lot of witches, even if they didn't exist until the hunt began. I like to use two flip charts and ask two members of the team to record group responses. One chart is labeled *Things Done Well* and the other *Things To Improve*. I then ask the group to brainstorm lists of these items, in any order, and the "scribes" capture them.

I *do not* like the approach in which one chart is labeled with a big plus sign and the other with a big minus sign. These still have the connotation of things done well (plus) and things done badly (minus), and things done badly will arouse defensiveness. In fact, even the words *things to improve* arouse a certain defensiveness.

If you don't believe this, consider your last performance appraisal. Most such appraisals begin with, "Well, Tom, you've done good work this past year. Here are some things I particularly want to commend you for." Now what do you think comes next? That killer word BUT! And following the killer word will be *helpful suggestions of things* for you to consider working on next year to improve your performance. Now think what is going on in your head. If you are honest with yourself, it might sound like this: "This jerk! He's saying I'm not doing well in this area. How dare he say that! I've been doing exemplary work in that area. I don't need to improve. He doesn't understand what I do!"

> **Principle:** No change takes place without feedback.
>
> **Principle:** If feedback is rejected, it is the same as if it were never received.

There is a principle of behavior change that says, no change takes place without feedback; the corollary to this rule is that if feedback is rejected, it is the same as if it were never received. So when you put people on the defensive, they tend to reject feedback that says something needs to change, and the net result is that the desired change never happens.

There are three rules that govern how often process reviews should be conducted. One is that they should occur at significant milestones in a project (usually when a major part of the work has been completed). However, a second rule is that they should be spaced no more than three months apart. This means that you may do process reviews between milestones. The reason for the three-month limit is that people seem unable to remember details for much longer, so if you go too long without one you lose important information. I would also suggest that reviews be conducted more frequently in the early stages of a team's development, and less frequently as it reaches maturity.

If you are doing a project that lasts only a few months, then you might want to do the process reviews every few weeks. Keep it "short and sweet." Generally, a review should take only about an hour maximum.

The third rule is that a process review should be conducted *after anything significant happens*. This is called the After Action Review (AAR) by the U.S. Army, and would be an excellent approach to use in project teams.

Process reviews can be moderated by the project manager, a team member, or an outside group facilitator (if you have one). There are pros and cons for all three. If the project manager conducts the audit, team members may not feel free to suggest improvements in her leadership methods. An outside facilitator or a team member can overcome this problem. However, an outside facilitator raises a new issue: Some teams don't want to air their dirty laundry in front of an outsider. My suggestion is that you do the reviews yourself the first few times, until you have developed a climate of openness and trust in the team; then you can invite an outside facilitator to come in.

Do select the outside facilitator with some care. Impress on that person that her role is not to find witches, but to help the team diagnose its processes.

## Using Interviews and Surveys

Gathering data for a process review can be done by interviewing team members individually or by having all of them fill out a questionnaire. The advantage of interviews is that with them you can get a greater depth of information than you can with a questionnaire. The disadvantage is that

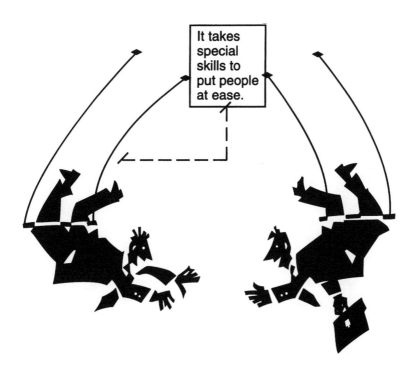

you might get nothing but pabulum if people don't trust you. It takes special skills to put people at ease so that they will be open and honest with you. Some people have that knack and others don't. So if you don't think you can get people to be candid with you, then a survey might be the only approach available to you.

At the end of this chapter is a questionnaire that I have used to get at process issues with teams. It has the advantage of anonymity and of being scaled. Although the scale numbers have no absolute meaning, you do get some idea of how strongly people agree or disagree with each item.

Once the data have been collected with this questionnaire, I summarize the information in histogram form, as shown in Figure 13-3. This tells how many people endorsed each point on the scale. Note that for this particular item, most team members are saying that they are pretty clear on the team's goals.

A second histogram is shown in Figure 13-4, this one for roles and responsibilities. In this case, we have what is called *bimodal split*. Half the team is saying that roles and responsibilities are not clear and the other half is saying that they are clear. Do you have a problem? You bet. This issue must be resolved.

> **Principle:** It makes no difference what is objectively true. People behave according to what they perceive to be true.

Note here that we are not concerned with whether the team's perception is objectively true. For all practical purposes, it makes no difference.

**Figure 13-3.** Team goals histogram.

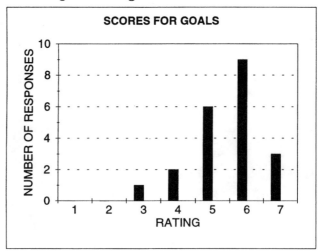

**Figure 13-4.** Histogram for roles and responsibilities.

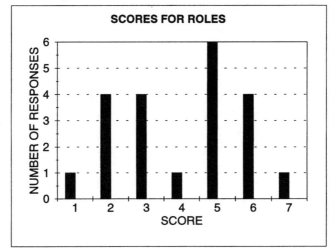

Perceptions govern behavior. So if they are all wrong in believing that roles and responsibilities are unclear, it makes no difference because they will behave as if it were true. So the rule is that we must deal with perceptions and correct them if they are wrong.

# Responding to the Data

Suppose your survey reveals that there is a lot of conflict in your team. There are also some problems with goals, roles, and procedures. You are especially concerned by the conflict, because this will interfere with the work. So you decide something should be done. You talk to someone in the company who suggests that you contact an outside consultant who specializes in conflict resolution. "Oh, sure, I can help you with that," says the consultant. "I recommend that we take your team to an offsite weekend retreat at Lake Wobegon. We can have Garrison Keillor in to tell a few stories for entertainment, and I'll facilitate a conflict resolution session. You'll be amazed at the results."

This sounds good. After all, the consultant has good references and speaks with authority, so you get the retreat idea approved. There is some complaining from team members about having to spend their weekend together, but you soften the blow with the Garrison Keillor carrot, and they go along with you because of the promise of fringe benefits (good food; some golf, perhaps; and Garrison).

To your delight, the conflict resolution session goes remarkably well. This consultant is definitely super! She really knows her stuff! At the end of the retreat, people are absolutely gushing with camaraderie and team spirit. This lady has definitely earned her consulting fee. You thank her profusely and go home, get a good night's sleep for the first time in weeks, and wake up the next day eager to get back to work.

Then, about three o'clock that day, the bomb drops! They are at it again—about to kill each other, in fact. They are accusing each other of having been total phonies at the retreat, of saying things they never meant, and are calling each other hypocrites and names not publishable in non-X-rated texts.

What happened?

What happened is that you made a fundamental mistake. While you noticed in your survey that people had concerns about team goals, roles and responsibilities, and procedures, you focused on conflict first—on the fact that there were problems with interpersonal relationships.

So what is wrong with that?

What is wrong is that conflict can be caused by the concerns people have about goals, roles, and procedures, and if you fail to address these first, the conflict will continue. For that reason, the operating rule is that you should deal with these in the following sequence:

1. Goals
2. Roles and responsibilities
3. Procedures
4. Relationships

To clarify this, think back to a time when you were in a team that was unclear about mission (goals). Or think of your project team when it was in the Forming stage of development. You hear people say, "I don't have a clue what we're supposed to be doing. I'm really frustrated!" And another person responds, "Oh, I'm pretty sure we're supposed to be doing xyz."

"Oh, no," someone else chimes in. "That's not it at all. You have it all wrong."

Next thing you know, they're all feeling angry with each other, and especially with you, the project leader.

The same thing happens if people are unclear about who is supposed to be doing what (roles and responsibilities). When you hear one team member ask another to do something and that person responds, "That's not my job," then you have a problem that we generally call *role conflict*. And this will lead to interpersonal conflict pretty fast.

So, again, you should deal with these four issues in a causal sequence, and if you do, you may find that the conflict goes away automatically, and if it doesn't, then you can work on conflict resolution and be fairly confident that the results will hold. Otherwise, you're just going around in a vicious circle.

## Do Something or Forget It!

The absolutely worst thing you can do is to conduct these reviews and then go on with business as usual. When you conduct process reviews, team members expect that something will be done to deal with the issues they have raised. Failing to do so simply tells them that the review was a waste of time, and they resent such a waste.

Once improvement issues are identified, a problem-solving session should be held to decide how to make the improvements. Further, as solutions are identified, members of the team should be given assignments to implement these solutions. It is best if these action assignments are taken on voluntarily, but it may be necessary to assign them yourself if no one volunteers.

You also need to make allowances for the time it takes people to carry out improvement work. They cannot be expected to do all of their project work *and* process improvement tasks besides if they are already fully loaded. This is one of the mistakes being made by organizations that are trying to reengineer their processes. They dump reengineering efforts on people who are already fully loaded with normal work, then wonder why *something* suffers.

## Sharing What You Learn

Although this may not apply directly to your team, I have found in my consulting work that teams seldom share what they learn with other teams. I have seen cases in which one team had made a mistake and learned about it, while another team in the company was repeating that very same mistake. This is a real waste.

The cost of learning should be incurred only once in any organization. Yes, I know it is painful to share your dirty laundry with those other teams. In fact, they are sometimes seen as the *enemy* because they compete for the same scarce resources as your team. Why, then, should you share anything with them that will help them perform better?

The answer is very simple. The word *organization* has the same root as the word *organism*, and indeed an organization is much like an organism. If any part of that organism is diseased, then it will eventually poison the entire system. So, from a systems perspective, anything I do to harm a part of my company will eventually come back to me, and conversely. For that reason, it is in my best interests to see that other project teams do not make the same mistakes we have made, and that they take advantage of the positive things we have learned as well.

The problem is that most companies have no mechanism in place for doing such team-to-team sharing. I would suggest that a quarterly meeting be held in which project teams present what they have learned in a time-limited format. People who want more information can always to go the team after the presentation. But this session should be clearly billed as an information-sharing event, not as an opportunity to throw rocks at anyone who "confesses a sin." Otherwise, it will die aborning.

## Barriers to Team Performance

There are a number of economic and social factors now entrenched in the United States that adversely affect teams. One is the spate of downsizings that has occurred in major corporations during the 1980s and 1990s. As Bill Hendrick, writing in the *Atlanta Constitution*, reports, downsizing breaks an unwritten social contract that will have a major impact on our culture over the long run. Dr. Catherine Daus, of the University of Southern Illinois, says, "We're hearing the term 'abandonment.' . . . This leads to all kinds of adverse effects: low self-esteem, self-destructive and antisocial behaviors" (Hendrick, 1996). When people realize that there is no such thing as a career path anymore—something many of them have counted on since high school—the result can only be cynicism, despair, mistrust, and anger.

The situation is worse than some people think. Sherwood Ross, of the *Pittsburgh Post Gazette*, writes that almost half of all employees worry about losing their jobs, and this fear is breeding a "me-first" attitude, making them suspicious and impairing their creativity. Fears of downsizing cause employees to view each other with suspicion. They may not stick a knife in someone's back, but they don't go out of their way to help others either. Certainly this has an adverse impact on team cooperation.

Furthermore, insecure employees tend to focus on politics, to look out for Number 1, rather than to cooperate with the team, and they rely on their own judgments more, and avoid risk. This risk aversion will reduce creativity (Ross, 1995).

Another major issue that affects teams negatively is job-family tension. As Gayle MacDonald reported in the *Toronto Globe and Mail*, "Job-family tension is *the* workplace issue of 1996, as it has been throughout the 90s'' (MacDonald, 1996). She goes on to say that ten years ago the home functioned as a haven. Now, however, the constant wear-and-tear on family relationships is taking a toll on business bottom lines because the employee's physical and mental health is being affected. For example, it is estimated that people with high levels of work-family conflict miss an average of eight workdays a year, compared to three days for people with low pressures.

## Taking Care of Employees

The good news is that more companies are offering some support. Many are becoming more accommodating to workers who need time off to take care of family matters (Mullins, 1995). In fact, it is futile to ignore the problem. As a staff report in the Rochester, New York, *Democrat and Chronicle* says, disregarding employees' lives outside the workplace causes personal problems that lead to ''half-people'' on the job. This was a finding of a Ford Foundation study. The report went on to say that changing how work gets done in order to help families also yields improved bottom-line results (*Democrat and Chronicle*, 1996).

In line with helping employees to deal better with their family responsibilities, many companies are finding that taking care of employees in general just makes good sense. As Rick Desloge, of the *St. Louis Business Journal*, reports, companies are finding that one of the best ways to satisfy customers is to first satisfy their employees (Desloge, 1996). This does not necessarily mean additional pay. Letting people participate in solving problems is more important, they find. Many successful companies are realizing that treating their employees like customers is a good approach.

# Finding Suitable Team Members

Another issue facing teams in the United States is the growing labor shortage. Demographers are forecasting that by the year 2000 we will create around 14 million new jobs, but our population will grow by only 12 million. That is a shortfall of 2 million workers. At the same time, predictions are that we will have a shortage of nearly 500,000 engineers.

Already we are feeling the crunch in many parts of the country. When unemployment levels reach 2.7 percent, it becomes very difficult to find employees, and this is true in Wisconsin, parts of Virginia, and other states in which I do consulting work. The fast-food restaurants are paying $6 to

$8 an hour and having trouble finding people to take those jobs. And one fellow told me that 40 percent of the people who apply for jobs at his company cannot pass the drug screening.

A vice president from a company in the Detroit area told me that they are already having trouble recruiting engineers. His company services the auto industry, and he said that the engineers he managed to find were soon lured away by the much higher salaries offered by the automakers. His solution is to recruit graduates from technical schools (two-year programs) and train them to do engineering work.

I am finding more and more companies facing similar problems. I believe there are some acceptable solutions, if they are applied correctly. One is aimed at the shortage of engineers. I believe that we should adopt the model used by the medical community for many years. A doctor delegates lab tests, inoculations, and other routine tasks to nurses and technicians. Doing so allows the physician to work at peak efficiency. Engineers should be able to do the same thing.

There is only one difficulty; for a long time we have been ignoring vocational education so that we are not turning out nearly enough technicians. The solution, I believe, is for companies to become more proactive in telling high school students about the available opportunities and perhaps offering scholarships to those who want to go to vocational school. This idea is a natural extension of the premise that if a company were having trouble obtaining raw materials, management would set about developing a source. Since people are major "raw materials" in many companies, then why not do the same thing with people?

## How to Manage Undiscussables

Chris Argyris, of Yale University, has found that in most organizations there are issues that cause problems that are undiscussable (Argyris, 1990). The phenomenon is similar to the Hans Christian Andersen story about the emperor who comes out to greet his subjects without any clothes on. Everyone is afraid to say anything except for a small child whose parents try desperately to hush him before the emperor hears what he is saying. They are afraid that if they call attention to the emperor's nakedness, he will respond by punishing them.

We fear similar fates in organizations. We all know that the CEO has a serious defect (I call these *character warts*), but no one is willing to call it to his attention. In fact, if anyone did, the possibility that the CEO might retaliate is very real. So we keep our mouths shut.

Furthermore, Argyris points out, the very fact that something like the

**Figure 13-5.** The left-hand column method at work.

**Purpose**

To help you become aware of the tacit assumptions that govern your actions.

**STEP 1: CHOOSE A PROBLEM**

Select a difficult interpersonal problem that you have had recently. Examples might include any of the following:

- You can't reach agreement with someone.
- Someone in your group is not pulling his or her own weight.
- You believe you are being treated unfairly.
- The team is resisting (or you believe it will resist) a change you think should be implemented.
- You are having difficulty getting your team to focus on a problem that you feel is critical.

Write a short paragraph describing the situation. What are you trying to accomplish? Who or what is blocking you? What might happen?

**STEP 2: THE RIGHT-HAND COLUMN (WHAT WAS SAID)**

Take several pieces of paper and draw a line down the center of each. Label the top of the left-hand column WHAT I'M THINKING and the top of the right-hand column WHAT IS SAID.

Now recall a frustrating conversation you have had about this issue, or imagine the conversation you believe you would have had if you had brought up the issue. In the right-hand column, write out the dialogue that actually occurred, or the one you believe would have happened if you had raised the issue. The dialogue may go on for several pages. Leave the left-hand column blank until you finish.

**STEP 3: THE LEFT-HAND COLUMN (WHAT YOU WERE THINKING)**

In the left-hand column, write out what you were thinking and feeling (but not saying) as the dialogue took place.

**STEP 4: REFLECTION: USING YOUR LEFT-HAND COLUMN AS A RESOURCE**

When you have finished writing out both columns, you may want to let the exercise cool for a few days before analyzing it. As you reflect on what is written, ask yourself:

- What really caused me to think and feel this way?
- What was my intention? What was I trying to accomplish?
- Did I achieve the results I wanted?
- How might my comments have contributed to the problem?
- Why didn't I actually say what is in my left-hand column?
- What assumptions did I make about the other person (or persons) involved?
- What must I believe in order to behave as I did in this situation?
- What were the costs of operating this way? What were the benefits?
- What kept me from acting differently?
- How can I use my left-hand column to improve my interactions and communications in the future?

*Source:* Adapted from the two-column research method developed by Chris Argyris and Donald Schön, *Theory in Practice,* San Francisco: Jossey-Bass, 1974.

CEO's character wart is undiscussable often becomes undiscussable itself, so there is no possible way that the problem will ever be solved.

Argyris has proposed a method of helping groups work on undiscussables that he calls the Left-Hand Column method. This method is shown in Figure 13-5. I suggest that you try this with your team only with the help of a skilled facilitator, because the process raises emotions that are potentially very explosive. It is a very useful device to try individually so that you can gain insight into your own hang-ups.

## Gathering Information on Processes

On the following page is a questionnaire you can use to identify process issues that should be addressed.

---

## The Team Performance Critique

*Instructions:* Indicate how you think the team is functioning by circling the number on each scale that you feel is most descriptive of the team.

---

### 1. Goals and objectives
Members do not understand
the goals of the team.

Team members understand
and agree on goals and objectives.

   1       2       3       4       5       6       7

### 2. Roles and responsibilities
Roles and responsibilities of team
members are not clear.

All team members are
clear about their roles.

   1       2       3       4       5       6       7

### 3. Procedures
Methods used to do our
work are inappropriate.

We follow sound work
methods and procedures.

   1       2       3       4       5       6       7

### 4. Relationships
Team members are often
in conflict.

Team members work
together harmoniously.

   1       2       3       4       5       6       7

### 5. Leadership
Team leadership is
often inadequate.

Team leadership is effective
and shared when appropriate.

   1       2       3       4       5       6       7

### 6. Planning
We have poor plans
for doing our work.

Plans are well
developed.

   1       2       3       4       5       6       7

### 7. Trust
People don't trust each
other on this team.

Members have a high degree of
trust in each other.

   1       2       3       4       5       6       7

### 8. Communications
Members don't communicate
with each other very well.

Communications are timely,
open, and appropriate.

   1       2       3       4       5       6       7

### 9. Creativity/Innovation
We live by the motto "If
it ain't broke, don't fix it."

We are willing to try
new ideas when they come out.

   1       2       3       4       5       6       7

---

# CHAPTER **14**

# Improving Your Communication Skills

No project manager can be effective if he or she has poor communication skills. But before effective communication can take place, certain basic conditions must be present. There must be a common culture between those doing the communicating and those receiving the communication. For instance, in communicating with nontechnical people, technically trained people must simplify their language, avoid jargon, and take the time to explain technical points. Communication also depends on having common expectations. When expectations differ, communication suffers. There must also be a willingness and motivation among all parties to communicate. You will have a hard time "getting through" to someone who has decided he or she doesn't want to hear what you have to say.

Once these conditions are met, there are five factors that affect whether a person is a good or poor communicator. These factors are self-concept, listening ability, clarity of expression, knowing how to cope with angry feelings, and self-disclosure (Bienvenu, 1971).

## Self-Concept

The most important factor affecting a person's communications with others is his self-concept. This is how a person sees himself. Every person has many concepts about himself involving who he is, what he stands for, what he does and does not do, what he values, what he believes, and so on. Most of us are extremely clear on some of these concepts, while others remain vague or fuzzy.

> **Principle:** The most important factor affecting your communications with others is your self-concept.

There are things that we know about ourselves and that others know about us. This is called our *public self*. There are also things about ourselves that we know but that no one else knows. This is called our *private self*. Then there is the *unknown self*—those aspects of ourselves that neither we nor others know about. Finally, there is the part that we don't know but that everyone else knows. We are *blind* to this part of ourselves.

A person's self-concept is formed early in childhood on the basis of what family members tell him about himself. If a child is told he is basically okay, that he can do whatever he sets out to do, then he will have a healthy self-concept. However, children told that they are not okay, and that they can't do a lot of things, tend to develop low self-esteem. As mentioned elsewhere in this book, when children have difficulty in school, American parents are inclined to attribute the problem to the child's native ability, whereas Asian parents are more likely to say that the child is not trying hard enough. This suggests that American children who have difficulty in school may have a lowered self-image compared with Asian children who experienced problems with their schoolwork.

In psychology, we have a model called *social comparison theory* that explains how we develop and maintain our self-concept. We compare ourselves with others throughout our lives to see how we stack up. If we seem about the same as or better than most people, then we have a positive self-image, with the reverse also being true. Our self-concept can change as we gain new life experience. So a person who begins with low self-esteem can gain new confidence through successful life experiences.

# Effective Listening

Much of communications skills training focuses on talking. There is not nearly enough emphasis on listening, even though the cause of many of our communication problems is our poor listening habits. An effective listener listens not only to the words spoken but to the *meaning* of the words. This includes understanding what the speaker is *feeling*. Not attending to the speaker's feelings can cause that person to feel unappreciated and misunderstood.

> **Principle:** An effective listener listens not only to the words but to the *meaning* of the words.

It is for this reason that we should practice *active* listening, as opposed to passive listening. Passive listening occurs when a person responds to the speaker by muttering uh-huh, nodding affirmatively, or saying, "I un-

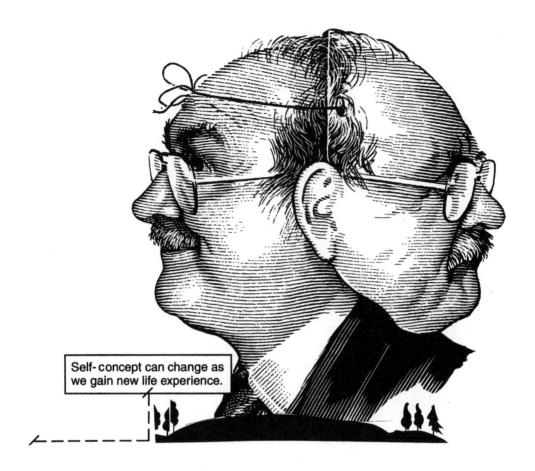

Self-concept can change as we gain new life experience.

derstand." But the speaker, faced with this response, has no way of knowing whether the listener really understands or simply thinks she does.

In active listening, the listener repeats back to the speaker what she has heard, but rephrases the content in her own words. If she simply parrots exactly the same words used by the speaker, it will seem that she understands even when she doesn't. For instructions on how to practice active listening, see Chapter 15.

There are two major reasons why people do not listen effectively. One is that they simply don't care what the speaker is saying. The other is that they are so busy thinking of a response to what the speaker has just said that they miss what the speaker is currently saying. Another reason for not listening effectively is that the listener is distracted by noises, activities nearby, or personal concerns. When it is important to listen, these causes should be eliminated. Get away from the noise or nearby activity if at all possible. If preoccupations with personal or previous concerns are keeping you from listening, then ask the speaker to meet with you later, after you have had a chance to deal with your concerns.

# Speaking Clearly

Some people seem oblivious to the fact that others do not understand them. They seem to think that because what they are saying is clear to themselves it must be clear to the other person. I have seen instructors respond to a question from a student by going back through their original explanation in the very same words they used the first time. It makes me want to say to them, "If those words had been any good, the student wouldn't have had a question. Change the way you present your explanation this time!"

There are some rules you should follow if you want to communicate effectively:

*Know what* outcome *you want to achieve.* Are you trying to inform? Get information? Give advice? Get someone to do something, change his behavior, or stop doing something? Are you trying to punish him verbally or shame him? Unless you are clear on your desired outcome, you may have trouble communicating effectively.

*Decide to* whom *you need to communicate.* Is it to the entire group? Or only to one person? It has always been a pet peeve of mine to see managers respond to some undesirable behavior on the part of one team member by writing a memo (or developing a written policy) to all group members telling them not to do what the offender did. In the first place, they probably have no intention of doing so; in the second, the memo to the group probably won't affect the behavior of the offender if she decides to misbehave again. The memo or policy is just a cop-out to avoid dealing face-to-face with the offender, and a manager who is afraid to confront employees who behave inappropriately should rethink his role.

*Determine the best mode in which to communicate your message.* Should it be written, verbal, or both? We know that putting things in writing can lead to future problems. This is especially true when you get angry about something and blast someone in writing. However, if you want to be sure that someone has clear instructions about something, then you might want to write them out.

*Have the sensory awareness to know when you get the response you want.* I have seen teachers who seemed completely unaware that people in their classes were totally lost. I have often thought that it would make no difference to them if the room were empty; they would still give their lecture, then pack up and go home. Clearly, you need to pay attention to your listeners when you talk and try to determine from their nonverbal responses if they are with you or not.

*Acquire* flexibility. Be able to vary your communication mode until you succeed in getting through to the other person. If you continue to repeat yourself, using the same words, you are deadlocked.

# Dealing With Anger

Sometimes we deal with our anger inappropriately and thus block communication with others. When I first entered the work force, I heard a manager tell someone to leave his feelings outside when he came to work. Yet he wanted that person to be motivated—and motivation is based on feelings or emotion. What he really wanted was for the person to leave his anger aside because he felt uncomfortable dealing with it.

The result of such a rule is that some people learn to suppress their anger for fear that others will think such behavior inappropriate. But they tend to save it up until one day the accumulated anger results in either an emotional explosion or a physical explosion in which the body literally "explodes" into a serious illness. Neither outcome is desirable.

Being able to express your feelings appropriately is necessary if you are going to have healthy relationships with others. Bienvenu (1971) offers the following suggestions for dealing with your emotions:

- *Be aware of your feelings.* When we are afraid of our emotions, we sometimes create a blind spot that keeps us from even knowing that we are feeling anything. If you have done this, it may take some time for you to regain your awareness.
- *Admit that you have feelings*—especially those considered bad or undesirable. We all have negative feelings sometimes. It is not human to be feelingless or to have only positive feelings. We aren't robots.
- *Accept responsibility for what you do with your emotions.* If you lash out at someone when you are angry, you must accept the consequences of that behavior.
- *Tell people how you are feeling.* Congruent communication requires that there be an accurate match between what you are experiencing and what you are saying.
- *Learn from understanding your emotions.* Ask yourself what caused you to feel as you did. Do this even with positive emotions.

# Self-Disclosure

If you want to have really good relationships and good communications with others, you must be willing to disclose things about yourself that help them to get to know you. This must be a mutual process, of course. If the other person is closed off, it will be hard to get to know him. The more we know about each other, the more effective our communications can be.

It is virtually impossible to know and relate to people who never let you know anything about themselves except for what is superficial. Unfortunately, in some companies there is such a climate of suspicion and fear that many employees do not want you to know them, and any attempt on your part to do so arouses their resentment. These individuals see your attempt to get to know them as a way of taking advantage of them.

As an example, a human resources manager told me about a manager in his company who wanted to enroll his children in a private school. Someone told him that a woman on the assembly line had placed her children in a school that interested him, so he went to talk to her. When he asked if it was true that she had her children in that school, her reaction shocked him. "It's none of your business," she said angrily, so he backed off. The next thing he knew, she went to HR and complained about this invasion of her privacy. In such settings, it is nearly impossible to get to know members of your teams.

# Content and Relationship

Every communication carries two components—the message or content of what you are saying and a definition of relationship with the person or group you are addressing. For example, suppose I say to someone, "Close the door." The content is clear. I want the door closed. The definition of relationship being expressed is one in which I feel it is okay to tell the person to do something and can expect her to do it.

> **Principle:** Every message carries both *content* and *relationship* components.

Contrast this with, "Please close the door." The content is the same, but the definition of relationship is different. We would say that in the first instance the relationship is one of unequal status, whereas the second suggests a more equal relationship. If the relationship is seen by both parties in the same way (either equal or unequal), then the definition offered will be accepted. However, if the other person sees the relationship as equal and you define it as unequal, then your definition will most likely be rejected.

All of us constantly deal with this definition of relationship issue whether we are conscious of it or not. Furthermore, it is impossible to communicate without offering a definition of relationship. For instance, have you ever been on a plane or bus and the person sitting beside you stared out the window and never once spoke to you? What did her silence convey to you about the way she viewed the relationship with you? Clearly, she did not want to engage you at all. She saw the relationship as nonexistent. So even silence communicates.

The technical terms for relationships are *complementary* and *symmetrical*. A complementary relationship is one of unequal status, whereas a symmetrical one is of equal status. It is interesting to note that symmetrical

When we communicate, we communicate the true meaning of a remark through the manner in which we do it.

relationships can be stable over the long term (on average, we might say), but they are unstable on a minute-to-minute basis. For example, my relationship with my wife might be symmetrical on average, but at any given moment she may "call the shots" and at another time I may do so. When she is calling the shots, the relationship is momentarily complementary, that is, of unequal status, and when I call the shots the same is true.

# Metacommunication

Not only do we define relationships when we communicate; we also communicate the true meaning of a remark through the *manner* in which we do it. This is called *metacommunication*. It is communication *about* the communication. As an example, suppose someone comes into my office and I say "Get out of my office" in an obviously joking way. The person knows enough not to take me seriously. This is the meta aspect of the communication. The fact that I have jokingly told her to get out of my office also defines our relationship as one in which we are very comfortable with each other and like to kid around.

Suppose, however, that I say "Get out of my office" in a way that sounds serious, and therefore I really mean that the words are to be taken at face value. The person turns around to leave. If I really mean for the person to leave, then the communication and metacommunication are congruent. However, if I don't really mean for her to leave, then the metacommunication is incongruent, and she will be totally confused.

It is also possible that I was joking but she thought I was serious. The other person always has to interpret the true meaning of a communication, and this is where difficulties can arise. If she misinterprets my meaning and gets angry, then I am going to have to repair the damage to our relationship, and this can sometimes be almost impossible if she is convinced that she understood my true meaning the first time round.

# Punctuating the Exchange Between Two People

Consider the following exchange that might take place when I try to talk to my friend who thinks I have thrown her out of my office.

**Boss:**   "Celia, I need to talk to you. When you came into my office earlier, I was just joking when I told you to get out."

**Celia:**   "Sure you were. You were serious, and you know it. I've never been so insulted in my life!"

**Boss:**    "Come on, Celia, you know I was just joking. I would never throw you out of my office. You're welcome any time."
**Celia:**   "Well, you sure sounded serious to me, and I think you're just trying to weasel out of it now."
**Boss:**    "You're being silly, Celia. You know very well I wasn't serious."
**Celia:**   "Well! Now you're calling me silly! I guess you don't want silly people in your office!"
**Boss:**    "Well, if that's how you see it, I sure don't!"
**Celia:**   "Fine!"
**Boss:**    "Fine!"

Now note what happened. If you asked Celia why she behaved as she did, she would tell you that she was only responding to my behavior. If you asked me why I behaved as I did, I would tell you that I was only responding to Celia's behavior. After all, she's the one who misunderstood and overreacted, I would tell you.

Thus, I see my behavior as a response to Celia's behavior, and she sees her behavior as a response to mine. In fact, there is a sense in which I see her behavior as *causing* mine, and she will say the same, that my behavior caused her to behave as she did. This is called punctuating the exchange, and is diagrammed as shown in Figure 14-1. I see the exchange as going 1-2-3, whereas Celia sees it as 2-3-4. In addition, once this exchange starts, it is very difficult to extinguish. It becomes what is called a *game without end*, but not in the fun and games sense. This is the essence of many conflicts and explains why they are so hard to resolve: Each side sees its behavior as a response to that of the other, and both will tell you, "I wouldn't have done what I did if he hadn't done what he did!"

**Figure 14-1.** Punctuation of communication.

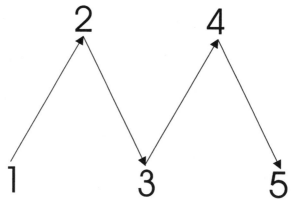

# Effect of Sensory Preferences on Communications

We gain knowledge of the world in which we live through the five senses. But most of us in fact prefer one of the five senses to the others and find that we gain knowledge and understanding more easily through that sense. In our society, the preferences tend to be for the visual, the auditory, and the kinesthetic (feelings), in that order.

Since individuals process information most efficiently when it is presented in the sensory system they prefer, you will find it helpful to notice which system they use and to communicate in it accordingly. Auditory people, for example, don't like to read long reports. A quick verbal summary suffices for them. Visual people, on the other hand, generally want pictures or diagrams to help them process information. And kinesthetic individuals want to *experience* it firsthand, preferring "walk-throughs" and other experiential ways of dealing with information.

If you add skills in detecting representational systems to those presented earlier in this chapter, you will find yourself communicating far more effectively.

### Exercise

During the next week, pay attention to how people express themselves using "I see," "I hear," or "I feel that. . . ." Try to respond by matching the sensory mode being used most often by the other person. This helps make your communications stronger.

## CHAPTER 15

# Dealing With a Team Member Whose Performance Is Unsatisfactory

It would be nice if managers never had to do anything but concentrate on getting work done. It would be especially nice if all employees did their jobs at the desired performance levels, had no performance deficits or bad work habits, and certainly no personality problems or bad attitudes. Unfortunately, that is not the case. Like it or not, every manager seems eventually to inherit a problem employee, and that is one reason the job gets tough. Problem employees can drain your energy and patience and tax your skills.

Most important for our purposes, problem employees can severely undermine teamwork. When employees refuse to cooperate, do not carry their share of the work load, cause conflicts with other team members, or have bad work habits, they can create real problems for the project manager. If such employees are not handled properly, the team may "go down the tubes."

## What Is a Problem Employee?

Before discussing how to handle problem employees, we first need to clarify what is meant by the term. We tend to view as a problem employee

Some of the material in this chapter was previously published in my book *How to Build and Manage a Winning Project Team* (AMACOM, 1994).

anyone who is significantly different from ourselves or who is unwilling to conform to conventional social expectations regarding dress or behavior. We sometimes want everyone to be part of a *herd*, although we euphemistically call it a team.

If this is our expectation, then we are in trouble as soon as we start dealing with artists, musicians, or technical people. Such people are very like to be "different," to say the least, and "nonconforming" in general. But these are not problems in themselves.

In actuality, an individual is only a problem employee if he or she:

- Interferes with the progress of work being done.
- Interferes with fellow employees in their work activities.
- Damages the image, reputation, or services of the company (Uris, 1988, p. 201).

So you have an employee who comes to work one day with a ring in his nose. He has always seemed a bit strange, but this is going too far! What do you do about him?

Does he fall into one of the three test categories? Does he interfere with the progress of work? No. Does he interfere with fellow employees in their work? Well, they stare at him and talk about him during breaks.

Some employees may be "different" and non-conforming in general, but their creativity and value to the company cannot be overlooked.

That's not sufficient. The interference is minimal and will probably die down in a few days as they become accustomed to his nose ring.

Does he damage the image, reputation, or services of the company? No. He goes to his work station, does his job, and has no contact with anyone outside the company. Of course, he probably tells people he works here, and they may wonder about us.

Again, that is not a big impact. Under these conditions, the person does not qualify as a problem employee.

Suppose, however, that as a sales representative for a pharmaceutical company he must call on physicians. He goes to work with his nose ring in place. In this case, if the doctors are offended by the salesman's appearance, he is damaging the image of the company and therefore constitutes a problem employee.

Now even though you may feel that people should have the freedom to choose their own lifestyles and dress, they must also accept the consequences of their choices, and since the choice being made by this individual will affect others, you have legitimate cause to intervene. Perhaps he can be transferred to a telephone sales job. Or perhaps he would be willing to limit his nose ring wearing to weekends and evenings, when he is not in contact with doctors.

So, to summarize, unless an employee does something that adversely affects the ability of an organization to perform, that person is not a problem employee.

# Pitfalls to Avoid

As I have said, dealing with a problem employee can be trying. It can take so much of your time that you begin letting important work slip, and you have no time left for your good employees. You may become a victim of the 80/20 rule, which says (in this case) that 80 percent of the time you spend dealing with team members will be spent with 20 percent of the team. And they will generally be the squeaky wheels that must be oiled. Of course, if you spend too little time with your good people, then the next thing you know is that *they* will develop problems.

The big pitfall is to invest too much effort in trying to save every problem employee. I am not saying that you shouldn't try to save them all; what I am saying is that there must be a limit to the effort you invest in any one person. Perhaps that sounds callous. I don't mean it to be. I simply recognize that there are limits to our ability to successfully turn all employees around. Here are some of those limits:

*Not everyone can be saved.* I know there are some managers who define as failure their inability to save all employees. However, you are being unfair to yourself if you look at it that way. Some problem employees may be suffering from deep-rooted psychological problems that require professional help. Not being a clinician, you aren't equipped to help. (And even the professionals have their share of failures. Behavioral "technology" is not so advanced that we can solve all psychological problems.)

*You don't have the time.* If you devote too much attention to one problem employee, you neglect the others, and soon their performance will begin to suffer. Further, you have only so much time to spend on employee problems. There is other work to be done, meetings to attend, deadlines to be met, and so forth.

*You probably don't have the skill.* No matter how much training you have had in dealing with people, you will still encounter those for whom you lack the specific skill needed. This may be one of the biggest traps: We keep thinking, "If I could just find the right approach, I could get this person to perform."

## Limits for Project Managers

When a project is organized hierarchically, that is, all the people on the team are "yours," then you can deal directly with problem employees. When the organization structure is a matrix, however, you must usually rely on functional managers to deal directly with such people. After all, the functional manager hired them, conducts their performance appraisals, and must deal with any performance problems they have.

This raises a very delicate issue. Project managers are ultimately responsible for the performance of all members of the team. However, they delegate some of that responsibility to functional managers in matrix proj-

Constant friction and turf battles create morale problems and lost time.

ects. If, for whatever reason, a member of a functional group is not performing satisfactorily, the project manager looks to the functional manager to get that person back on track. If this does not happen, then the project manager will have to intervene. Then you have the potential for a turf battle.

This can be a very explosive issue. Functional managers sometimes protect marginal employees. They may do so for a number of reasons, ranging from friendship with the employee, to being blackmailed, to being too lazy to take the time to correct the problem, to not knowing how, to being blind to the problem. For whatever reason, the functional manager will resent a project manager's suggesting that the person is not performing satisfactorily.

What is especially awkward is that the project manager may not be able to objectively evaluate the person's performance. As an electrical engineer, I will have difficulty evaluating the performance of a mechanical or chemical engineer. So again, I have to rely on functional managers to evaluate the quality of work being done by members of their groups.

When the problem is with the person's work habits, rather than his technical performance, however, you may have to intervene yourself. For example, he comes in two hours late every other day and always leaves at quitting time. He is supposed to be spending full time on your job. You know he isn't, yet he charges forty hours to the project every week, and he is getting behind schedule, which will adversely affect the project eventually.

Or perhaps he comes to team meetings and reads a magazine, never gets involved, just uses the meeting as an opportunity to goof off. Or he goes around rabble-rousing. He complains to other team members about how you treat him, how you manage the project, the "unrealistic" schedule, and whatever else he can find to complain about. Soon you have morale problems with your team.

> **Premise:** You must have the right to remove from your project any member who does not perform—for whatever reason—or you cannot be held accountable for performance outcomes.

You talk to his boss, who defends him. What do you do then?

My position is that you must have the right to remove from your project team anyone who cannot or will not perform or who falls into the definition of a problem employee, for whatever reason.

I understand the limits of what I am saying. I have been there. I also know that some people will again think I am being very callous. So be it. I have experienced the very detrimental effect such people can have on all my other team members, and I am convinced that I must balance my desire to be fair with the employee with the same desire to be fair to the majority of my team.

Even when the functional manager is sympathetic to your problem, there will be times when she will tell you, "He's all I have. Take him or leave him."

Then you may have to go to your boss and ask for help. Perhaps you can bring in a contract employee. Perhaps your boss can intervene and get the functional manager to move several people around.

It may be, in some cases, that the employee works well for other project managers but not for you. It may really be a personality clash. In that case, moving people around is fine. (I do have problems, however, with passing an incompetent employee off onto someone else just to solve my problem.)

Whatever the case, it is important that such situations be handled as quickly, as compassionately, and as quietly as possible. Failure to take action quickly can undermine your position later. A move that seems callous may undermine the morale of the team. And letting the situation explode can only make life difficult for everyone.

I do have one concern. It is easy in a project to be blackmailed. You have a tight deadline. The employee is very marginal, yet he is all there is available. Rather than take him off the project, you try your best to deal with him. You can't recruit anyone else because you have him on the team. In the final analysis, you will be held accountable for performance when you could not manage it, so you are better off taking your lumps now than you are postponing a resolution of the situation until later. Get the person off the team and then find a replacement if at all possible.

# Dealing With Pathological Problems

Managers can be equipped to deal with performance deficits, poor work habits, interpersonal conflicts, and so on. However, employees sometimes have serious pathologies that require professional help to resolve. These include alcoholism and drug problems as well as such things as chronic lying, refusing to abide by rules, and schizophrenia and other psychological disorders.

The problem for many managers is that the behavior appears to be just a "personality thing," or it may be defined as just "poor work habits." So the manager engages in coaching and counseling, but no progress is made. When you find yourself dealing with pathology, you need help. If your personnel department cannot give it to you, you may need to consult with a professional outside the workplace who can advise you.

I know of a manager who was unaware that one of her employees had recently had a nervous breakdown. She gave him a mild reprimand for some performance problem, after which he had a relapse. Later he sued the company. They settled out of court, but it was a traumatic experience for the manager.

If you believe you are dealing with pathological problems, get professional help! Don't try to carry the burden alone.

# Skills for Dealing With Problems

You must have a handful of skills before you can deal effectively with problem employees. These include the ability to:

- Listening actively.
- Describe behavior without interpreting intentions.
- Give and receive feedback.
- Resolve conflict.

## Active Listening

In the sixteen years that I have been teaching interpersonal skills, I have found active listening to be one of the hardest skills to teach. In its essence, it is simplicity itself—you simply summarize what you hear someone else say. You do so periodically, saying in your own words what you have heard so that the person speaking can tell that you are listening to understand.

The difficulty is that people think if they periodically ask questions of the other person that this is active listening, but it is not—it is interviewing, and there is a significant difference! When someone listens to you and signals that she is doing so with head nods and expressions of "I understand," you really have no way of knowing for certain that she does in fact understand. On the other hand, when she says, in her own words, what she heard you say, then you at least know that she has heard you and is trying to understand.

This is a very important approach because it is essential in dealing with an interpersonal problem of any kind that the other person know you are trying to understand her position. Otherwise, she may feel that you are only trying to push your own points without really understanding her position.

It requires a lot of practice to be able to do active listening in the right way. If you reflect back too often, the person begins to feel frustrated. If you use the exact words of the other person, rather than rephrasing, she will think you are condescending. So achieving balance is very important. The beauty of this skill is that, once you master it, you can use it in virtually every communication you have with someone else.

## Describing Behavior

Another skill that is important in dealing with a problem employee is to be able to describe his behavior without drawing conclusions about what his motives are. Suppose, for example, that someone frequently interrupts you. The behavior prompts you to think that the person does not want to hear what you have to say. This may not be the case. The person may simply be so excited that he can't wait to express his own thoughts. Yes, he is being rude, but the *cause* may not be what you think it is.

Drawing conclusions about the causes of someone's behavior is mind reading, and most of us resent having others attribute motives to us that are not correct. So in giving someone feedback (which is discussed in the next section), you should begin by describing his behavior, with no comment about what you believe his motives are.

To teach this skill, I simply have people watch a person move around and tell me what they see him doing. If he scratches his head and someone says; "He has an itch," I remind the observer that this is an inference. All you can say is that he scratched his head. He may not have an itch at all (indeed, in this situation, he probably does not).

## Giving and Receiving Feedback

In the following table are guidelines on giving someone feedback. A couple of comments are in order. The table says that feedback should be given as soon as possible after the behavior occurs. However, you are to understand that this means in an appropriate setting. If the incident happens in a meeting, you should *not* give the person feedback in front of others.

| Guidelines for Giving Feedback | |
|---|---|
| Effective | Ineffective |
| Should describe the person's *behavior*. | Guesses at the person's *motives*. |
| Should be given as soon as possible after the behavior occurs. | Delayed until a later time, so the person's memory is no longer fresh. |
| Tell how you felt about the behavior—you were angry, sad, upset, worried. | Keep your feelings to yourself. |
| Most effective when several people tell the person. (However, don't gang up on him or her.) | Least effective when only one person gives the feedback. It may only be that person's perception, not the reality. |

It is also appropriate to tell the person how you felt about his behavior. Some of us have been taught not to talk about our feelings—as if it were inappropriate to have them—but I think it is important for others to know the impact of their behavior. If I were not having an emotional response to someone's behavior, it would not be an issue in the first place.

Also, as the table indicates, feedback is most effective when it comes from several someones, but this doesn't mean you should get a group together to confront someone. It just happens that if only one person tells you he doesn't like something you do, you can discount it, but if several people tell you, the criticism becomes harder to ignore.

When you deal with others, there may be times when they say that something you are doing is a problem for them. In this case, you should know how to receive feedback, and this approach is outlined in the next table.

| Guidelines for Receiving Feedback | |
|---|---|
| Effective | Ineffective |
| Listen *actively* to understand. | Listen only to rebut what the other person tells you. |
| Ask questions to clarify. | Be passive. |
| Check to see if others agree. | Accept one person's comments as if they are absolutely true. |
| Reserve your autonomy. You don't have to change just because others may not like what you do. | Cave in to group pressure. |

## Dealing With Conflict

Managing conflict will be covered in detail in Chapter 16. Before you try confronting an employee, you should read that chapter.

## A General Approach to Dealing With Problem Employees

Following is a structured procedure for dealing with a person who is not performing satisfactorily. It will usually be used only when the employee reports directly to you. If the person is in a functional group, then the functional manager should deal with her. If that manager does not know this procedure, you might share it with him.

*Identify the unsatisfactory performance in behavioral terms.* When dealing with employees on some aspect of their performance or personal behavior, stick with the actual *behavior* that is the problem. Avoid making comments about their bad *attitude*, lack of motivation, and so on. When you suggest that an employee has a bad attitude or is unmotivated, you are mind reading, as I explained previously under the skill of describing behavior.

Your inference about attitude is based on your observation of the person's *behavior* and is indeed a conclusion on your part. You may be correct in your conclusion; on the other hand, you may not. Either way, you will only know if a person's attitude has changed, or his motivation has improved, when his behavior changes, so go for a change in behavior from the start.

> **Premise:** The only way you know that someone has a good or bad attitude is by observing his behavior, so work on changing behavior, not minds!

Let me illustrate this with a story told me by a manager. An employee who worked for one of her supervisors came to the manager and asked to talk. He told the manager, "I want to know why I can't get promoted in this group. I've been here as long as Charlie and I do as good work as he does, but he got promoted and I didn't when I got my last review."

"Have you talked with your supervisor about it?" the manager asked.

"No, I didn't think it would do any good."

"Well, you raised the issue, and I don't know all the facts, so I'll have to get him in here and we'll talk about it," the manager replied.

She called the supervisor in. The supervisor looked surprised to see the employee sitting there.

"He wants to know why he can't get promoted," the manager explained to the supervisor.

The supervisor didn't hesitate. He looked directly at the employee and said, "Well, frankly, it's because you have a bad attitude."

The employee's reaction is easy to imagine. The manager said he turned red and probably would have slugged his supervisor if he could have got away with it, but before he could say anything, the manager interrupted.

"Hold on a minute," she said. And to the supervisor, "Tell him what he does that causes you to say that."

"Oh, well, sometimes I give you a job that you think you shouldn't have to do and you go around and complain to the other guys in the group and, next thing I know, I have a morale problem with the group."

The manager asked the employee, "Is it true that you sometimes do this?" (Note that she gave the employee some latitude to save face, without letting him off the hook entirely.)

The employee fidgeted, then said, "I guess so."

"Can you see why this is a problem for your supervisor?"

He could.

"Will you agree that if you want to get promoted, this is something you will have to stop doing?"

She got the employee to agree. Then she asked what else he did that caused problems for the supervisor. There were a couple of minor things. She got the employee to agree to change, and eventually he was promoted.

In this situation, I would agree that the employee probably had a bad attitude. He felt that some jobs were beneath him and should be given to a more junior person. I call those undesirable jobs "toilet-cleaning jobs." Most people don't want to do them, but we all have to take them on occasionally. This employee felt he shouldn't have to do any of them.

Nevertheless, to tell him that he has a bad attitude gets you nowhere. In the final analysis, all you care about is a change in his behavior, so that is what you should deal with from the start.

Now for the questions you must ask and answer before acting:

*Does the person know that his performance is unsatisfactory?* Managers sometimes make an error here in assuming that the employee knows his performance is below par. However, employees do not always know how to judge their own performance. Unless the manager has told them exactly what is expected and how they will be measured, they cannot be expected to know.

*Does the person know what to do and when?* Even managers have problems with priorities sometimes. Quality control experts caution us to be careful not to get trapped into letting the "trivial many" things keep us from attending to the really important "vital few" tasks. Think about it. When were you ever instructed in school on how to do work planning? If the subject were taught in school, all these courses in managing time would have no market. So we may have to help some of our people learn how to get organized.

*Are there obstacles outside this person's control?* It is possible for there to be problems caused by organizational systems that prevent employees from performing up to their potential? Managers sometimes overlook these. J. M. Juran and other quality gurus have been saying for years that we must attend to management-controllable factors before addressing employees. To tell an employee to "do it right the first time," when the tools, equipment, or system make it impossible for her to do the job will get you nowhere and will only cause the employee to resent your badgering.

*Does this person know how to do the job?* What kind of training has the person had? If he was trained by another employee, you cannot be sure that the trainer didn't pass on bad practices to the trainee. I have heard stories of employees who were confronted by their bosses because they were doing the job wrong and the employee said, "That's how I was taught to do it," and when the manager checked, he found that the employee was right.

Just because a person is good at doing a job does not mean that he can teach it to others. In fact, some of the most brilliant minds have difficulty explaining to others what they do. The task is so easy for them that they cannot understand why anyone would have trouble with it. So it is a good idea to check out how training is being done before you trash the employee.

*Is the person penalized for performing well?* This can happen unwittingly. Sometimes a really good employee is "rewarded" for her good performance by being given more and more work until she becomes so overloaded that she can no longer perform. It is natural to depend on our best employees, but we must be careful not to load them so heavily that they are unable to carry the weight.

Another way employees are sometimes penalized is by the group itself. If a team member does more work than the other members feel is fair, they may call him a "rate-buster" and put pressure on him to slow down; otherwise he will make the rest of them look bad. Such incidents are most likely to occur on construction projects in which unions are concerned that their employees not be taken advantage of by management, so they establish norms about how much work a person should do during the day. In this case, the suggestion is to remove the penalty or transfer the person to a job in which there are no such penalties. If it is a rate-busting situation, you won't be able to do this.

*Is the person rewarded for nonperformance?* This can be the reverse of the rate-busting case. Other team members urge the employee to slack off. They may also play a game which in transactional analysis is called "let's you and him fight." They want the employee to aggravate the team leader until it becomes a fight; then they sit on the sidelines and laugh. They don't care who wins. The fight is reward enough.

There are subtler ways that employees are rewarded for nonperformance, and these may not be easy for a manager to detect. If the employee has a problem with authority figures, he may perform inadequately as a way of rebelling against the authority you represent. This is an example of a pathological problem, one that you are not likely to be able to handle. Such situations can be very trying and may eventually require you to remove the person from your team.

*Does the person have the potential to do the job if he wanted to?* Sometimes we find that the employee simply doesn't have the ability to perform. In such cases, we certainly want to avoid penalizing this person for something he can't help. After all, it may have been the manager's error in hiring him in the first place.

Usually, organizations can find a slot for an employee in another group, a job for which the person has potential, not just a job to which you can transfer him in order to get him out of your hair. If that is possible, the employee can be transferred. If no such job exists, then I personally feel the organization should try to help the employee find a job elsewhere and not just terminate him.

If the answer to this question is that the person does have the potential to do the job, then you as manager need to counsel this employee. It may be that coaching will solve the problem. However, it may turn out that while the person *could* do the job, she has no motivation to do it. In that case, either the person should be transferred to a job for which she does have motivation or a way must be found to get her turned on to the present job.

# Changing Behavior

When you reach the last step in the model, where you are coaching the employee to try to get her to perform acceptably, you are attempting to change her behavior. If you have ever tried to do this with another person or even yourself, you know how hard this can be. Yet it is necessary that we get people to change when their performance is unacceptable; otherwise, it is impossible to get project work done on time and within budget.

The steps involved in changing behavior are fairly well understood. In Figure 15-1 is a model that I have adapted from Marvin Weisbord (1987) and that illustrates the steps involved. This does not make the steps easy, however.

Weisbord writes that people live in various rooms of a four-room house. So long as everything is going along alright, they tend to live in the room called contentment. In this state, there is no reason to change. Everything is great. If that is really the case, fine, but when problems exist, this would be called complacency. Teams and organizations sometimes get into this position because of previous successes. In our case, we are dealing with an employee whose performance is not acceptable, and if we are following Fournies' model, we have told him. When we do so, how do you think he will respond? You guessed it! He moves into denial!

**Figure 15-1.** The four-room house model.

*Source:* Adapted from Marvin Weisbord, *Productive Workplaces* (San Francisco: Jossey-Bass, 1987).

## When Denial Sets In

This is not a universal response when someone is confronted with a performance problem, but it is fairly often the case. When people move into denial, it sounds like this: "I don't have a problem," they say. "You're being unfair. My work is as good as that of so and so."

Often they blame everyone else. Comedian Flip Wilson used to have the typical response, "The devil made me do it."

> **Premise:** So long as a person stays in denial, his behavior is almost guaranteed not to change.

This is the real block managers must deal with. Getting an employee out of denial can be extremely difficult. So far as the person is concerned, she does not have a problem. You are being unfair. Other employees perform exactly the same. "Why are you picking on me?" she complains.

One of the basic premises of Alcoholics Anonymous is that until a person admits he has a drinking problem, he can't be helped. And most alcoholics are in a state of denial when first confronted with the problem by family and friends.

This can be illustrated with a work example: A project manager hired an engineer to do design work. The engineer had formerly worked for a very prestigious company, and he gave a very impressive interview. What the manager failed to realize was that the engineer had been in a job that required very good analytical skills. The design job, however, required good synthesis skills. Needless to say, the engineer's design work was not up to par.

The manager tried to help the engineer by instructing and working with him, trying to teach him to do better design. It was no use. The engineer lacked an innate ability to do conceptual work, and so the manager finally had to confront him. The engineer immediately went into denial, insisting that the manager was being unfair.

Then another project got behind schedule and the engineer was transferred temporarily to that job. He worked on it for a while, the crisis ended, and he returned to his original job. His work was still unsatisfactory, and because most of his work had to be redone he was missing deadlines.

The project manager offered to transfer the engineer to another group in which he would have been doing essentially the same work he had done for his previous employer, work that required good analytical skills. But the engineer would have no part of this. He saw it as a demotion. Further, it would be admitting that he lacked design skills.

Finally the project manager could not tolerate the situation any longer. He was being held accountable for meeting deadlines and it was impossible to do so with an incompetent engineer. So the department manager got the two project managers for whom the engineer had worked into his office, together with the errant engineer, to decide what to do.

The engineer was still in denial. He blamed the first project manager for all his problems. Finally, he said, "I did good work for Bob, didn't I?"

Bob, who was the other project manager, happened to be a very kind-hearted fellow who hated to trash anyone, but he was backed up against a wall. After some moments, he said, "Frankly, no, you didn't."

The engineer was crushed. He was now being told by two managers that his work was unacceptable. He was in the panic room.

The department manager again offered to transfer him, but he was offended and refused. "Then you had better start looking for another job," the department manager told him. They gave him three months grace, and he was able to resign without any black marks going on his record.

This case was handled as humanely as possible because the manager who hired the engineer had made an error in judgment. Note, however, that the employee was never got into renewal. He was not salvageable because his behavior was not something that was under his control.

In cases in which the person does have control over his or her behavior, if you can just move them into the panic room, you can usually get them into renewal. Then the individual can move back into contentment. The following procedure explains how to accomplish the steps needed to move the individual through the four rooms.

1. *You must challenge the person's model of reality so strongly that he is "unfrozen."* That is, he must agree that his model is defective. This is done by presenting the person with evidence to show that he is not performing properly. This will move the person from contentment to panic if you are successful.

2. *You must offer a new model that is consistent with the majority view and can be expected to lead to more positive behavior.* To say this in simpler terms, you must tell the employee specifically how you want him to behave. Don't assume he knows. Outline it as precisely as you need to in order to show the person what is required.

> **Principle:** Before a person will change, he must be unfrozen. That is, he must see a need to change.

3. *Induce the person to try new behavior that is consistent with the new model.* In other words, get him to perform as you have outlined in step 2.

4. *You must reward the successful performance of the new behavior* so that the new behavior is adopted permanently. As soon as there is movement in the right direction, let the person know that you have observed it and are pleased by it.

Let me illustrate that this approach works with an anecdote told by Dr. Milton Erickson, who was one of the nation's preeminent psychiatrists before his death a few years ago. Dr. Erickson told about a fellow whom he called Joe, whose parents committed him to the state reformatory when he was twelve years old. Now it is one thing to have the law do this, but when parents send a child to the state reformatory, something extreme must be going on.

Indeed there was. Joe happened to be a fairly large boy for his age, and he delighted in picking fights with other kids, and because of his size he generally beat them up, and their parents would then complain to Joe's parents about his behavior. That alone would be bad enough.

But Joe did really bizarre things.

He stabbed his father's cow with a pitchfork and nearly killed it.

He set the barn on fire.

He would pour kerosene on dogs and cats and then set them on fire. He thought this was great fun.

Clearly, Joe was a very sick child.

Finally, his parents decided that they could not manage him, and they turned the problem over to the state.

Joe stayed in the reformatory until he was twenty-one. Then the state had to release him because he was no longer a juvenile. He was out of the reformatory only a few weeks before he committed a felony, was caught, and was sentenced to prison.

He no sooner got to prison than he got into a fight with another inmate, and as punishment he was placed in solitary confinement.

In those days (the 1920s), prison conditions were pretty bad and solitary confinement was called the dungeon, because it was in the basement. As a rule, the punishment was considered so severe that most prisoners behaved after serving their term in solitary.

Not Joe.

He no sooner got out than he got into another fight.

Back to solitary he went.

He did the same thing again when he got out—got into a fight.

The problem here is that if you stay in solitary too long your muscles atrophy, so they have to take inmates out periodically for exercise. Every time, Joe would get into a fight.

The prison officials finally decided to let him out only at night, when everyone else was sleeping. Now he would fight with the guards.

The net result was that he spent most of his prison term in the dungeon.

Then he was released.

He was out no time at all when he committed another felony. Back to the state prison he went.

He spent most of this term in the dungeon as well.

Now you don't have to be a psychiatrist to make an accurate prediction about Joe, do you? He will spend most of his life in prison, if he doesn't kill someone and get the death penalty.

He is finally released from his second prison term and goes back to his hometown. By this time, his parents have passed away, the farm has been sold, and so Joe has nothing to his name except the suit of clothes and $15 given him by the prison.

He spends several days just loafing around town, doing nothing.

Or, at least, it appeared he was doing nothing.

However, a motorboat motor is missing and a store has been broken into and the cash drawer emptied. The coincidence with Joe's arrival is unmistakable, but the local police have no proof, so they just wait for him to make a bad move.

On the third or fourth day in town, Joe is sitting on a bench on the sidewalk, when he sees a very attractive young woman approaching. Her name is Edie, and she is unmarried. Joe gets up, steps in front of her, and blocks her path.

She stops and looks up at him.

"You want to go to the dance with me Friday night?" Joe says.

Edie doesn't blink an eye. Very quietly she says, "If you're a gentleman, I will."

With that, Joe steps aside and Edie goes on with her shopping.

On Friday night, Joe goes to the local barn dance, and in due time Edie appears. Joe asks her to dance, and she dances with him. By the end of the evening, she has danced almost every dance with Joe.

Now this is a small farm town, where everyone knows everyone and everything that is going on, and no doubt people were wondering about Edie. After all, this guy was a common criminal. Lands! Surely Edie should know better than to associate with such as him!

Next day, Saturday, the money reappears in the cash drawer and the motor boat motor finds its way back home.

And Joe walks out of town to Edie's farm and finds her father, who is working in the fields.

"I'd like a job working on your farm," Joe tells her father.

Her dad looks him up and down, no doubt aware of his background. "Farming is hard work, boy," he says. "I don't think you'd like it."

Joe was not to be dissuaded. "I'd like to give it a try," he said.

"Got no place for you to sleep except in the barn," her father says.

"No problem," says Joe. "I'd like a chance."

"Can't pay you but $15 a month."

"That's fine."

Apparently her father found something convincing in Joe's manner. Or perhaps he just decided to let Joe see for himself how hard farming is, so he told him okay, he would give him a chance.

To the astonishment of everyone who knew him, Joe turned out to be a model farmhand. He worked harder than anyone. He never complained about anything. When neighbors were sick, he even volunteered to help them with their chores.

Most important, he married Edie, moved out of the barn into the house, and never got into any more trouble.

Now I must remind you that this is a true story. Dr. Erickson did not make it up. He used it in the same way I have, to illustrate a profound example of behavior change, one that all the experts would have predicted would never happen.

But it did.

The question is whether we can learn anything from this example that can be applied to changing behavior in general, and the answer is yes.

The model presented above fits perfectly. Joe was unfrozen by his desire to spend time with Edie.

She gave him a new model—he had to be a gentleman if he wanted to spend time with her.

She got him to behave differently at the dance, although no doubt he was a bit rough around the edges.

He was rewarded by getting to spend the evening with Edie, and this moved him to change.

Now let's look closely at the situation. No doubt Joe was not the ideal gentleman initially. This in itself is significant. You have to accept people where they are initially, then gradually move them closer to where you want them to be. I expected that Edie occasionally had to say to Joe, "A gentleman wouldn't do that."

Another vital point is in how he was rewarded. At the surface level, it was by getting to spend the evening with Edie. However, there is a much deeper, more significant level on which he was rewarded, and that was in knowing that he was beating the competition for Edie's attention.

Consider this: Joe was now doing what he had always done, but in a socially acceptable way. He was beating the other guy, but not by bashing him. And this illustrates one of the most important principles of changing behavior. No behavior in and of itself is good or bad—it is the consequence of the behavior that we label good or bad. So, if you can redirect so-called bad behavior so that it has a positive outcome, then you will find changing behavior to be easier than if you expect a radical

> **Principle:** No behavior in and of itself is good or bad. It is the result that we call good or bad. If behavior can be redirected to get a positive outcome, rather than a negative one, behavior *change* is easier.

change. As an example, remember our devil's advocate in the chapter on meetings? We simply redirected the person's behavior to get a positive outcome rather than a negative one.

This by no means makes it easy. If it were easy, we would have no behavioral problems anywhere, but we do.

## Exercises

1. If you are having a problem with a member of your team, go through the flow chart and decide how you should handle it. Begin by describing the behavior that is a problem for you. Do not draw conclusions about what his or her motives or attitudes are. That is mind reading.
2. Describe to a colleague the problem person's behavior and have this colleague play the part of the team member. You should try to correct the problem. By practicing like this in a ''safe'' manner, it should be easier when you actually confront the problem person.

NOTE: If your company is paranoid about being sued, you should follow company policy in dealing with any problem team member. Some companies require that you not confront an employee unless a member of the human resources department is present.

# CHAPTER 16

# Managing Conflict in Project Teams

Some people think that conflict in an organization is to be avoided at all costs. But the fear and avoidance of conflict can sometimes result in problems that are more serious than the existence of conflict itself. In this chapter we will examine the causes of conflict and how to manage or resolve conflict when it turns destructive.

## Strategies for Dealing With Conflict

There are two basic conflict strategies that a manager must apply in an organization. The first is to *manage conflict* so that differing ideas, opinions, and approaches are brought out for discussion and handling. The second is to *resolve conflict* when it becomes interpersonal.

We must have conflict of ideas if we are to have creative capacity in organizations. We must also know when people disagree with us, or we will never reach a point at which we can get their full commitment to and support for vital programs.

However, conflict of ideas may lead to interpersonal conflict, and when this happens, it must be resolved, or damage to the effective functioning of the organization will result. Such conflict must be *confronted*, and herein lies one of the more common causes of difficulty in many groups. The manager hopes the conflict will "go away." It seldom does. Usually it just festers underground until pressure builds up to the point of explosion. Then the manager has a crisis to deal with.

Conflict occurs when a person or group frustrates the concerns of another person or group.

# Causes of Conflict

Conflict occurs when a person or group frustrates the concerns of another person or group. Conflicts arise over the following concerns:

- *Values.* These are what we deem basically important. They may include our work ethic, our sense of family responsibility, etc.
- *Facts.* Not all team members will necessarily have the same perception of what the facts are. The reality of one faction may clash with the reality of others.
- *Role perceptions.* People on teams often have different views of each other's roles, and this can lead to *role conflict.* Such conflict can be resolved through role negotiation.
- *Methods.* We disagree about the best or right way to go about individual tasks or the project as a whole.
- *Objectives.* There are two sources of conflict involving objectives. One is over what the objectives should be. The other is over which objectives should take priority.

# Approaches to Conflict

There are five approaches to conflict—win-lose, win-win, compromise, accommodating, and avoidance. The method you choose depends on how you answer the following two questions:

1. How strong is my concern for satisfying my own interests in this issue?
2. How strong is my concern for satisfying the interests of the other party?

This is shown in graphic form in Figure 16-1. A *win-win* approach is generally considered the most preferable one for all the parties concerned. However, we are often socialized into adopting a *win-lose* approach. This is the competitive posture and is based on the view that there must be a winner and a loser. In sports, we often do not permit a tied game. One side *must* win. This is called a zero-sum game. The pie must be divided, and if one

**Figure 16-1.** Five approaches to conflict.

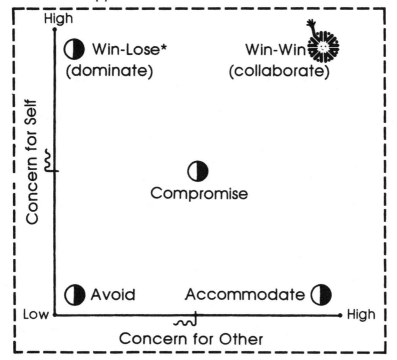

*Tends to become lose-lose.

side gets a big share, only a small one or nothing will be left for the other side.

The *compromise* position is often considered the only way in which a conflict can be resolved. However, compromise always leaves both sides feeling a bit cheated (that is, when it is a true compromise). This is because both parties give up valued outcomes, and negative effects always weigh heavily on the mind, so that each party tends to focus on what it has lost rather than on what it has gained.

> **Premise:** A win-lose approach often turns into lose-lose. The smart negotiator will attempt to move win-lose situations toward win-win or at least toward a compromise position.

*Accommodating* occurs when you are more concerned with meeting the needs of the other party than your own. For example, suppose I have had a really rough day and come home dead tired, but my child says, "Dad, can you take me to the soccer game?" I haven't spent much time with him lately, so I say, "Sure, let's go."

*Avoidance* is really not dealing with conflict at all. It may be all right to avoid conflicts when the issues really aren't very important. If they are important, however, avoiding is a problem, since the issue never gets resolved.

# Suggestions for Handling Conflict

The following techniques can be used in most conflict situations:

*Choose a neutral setting in which to discuss the problem.* Your office is not the best place because it automatically puts the other person at a disadvantage.

*State your sincere desire to resolve the conflict to the satisfaction of both parties.* (If you want to trash the other person, perhaps you should wait until you have cooled off before you begin. You can't fake it. If you want to stomp your opponent, it will come out sooner or later.)

*Do not assume that you know the other person's motives, intentions, thoughts, or feelings.* To do so is mind reading and only aggravates the conflict.

*Deal with the issues, not the character of the person.* Remember, you want a change in the person's behavior, not the person himself.

*Where value differences have caused the conflict, deal with the tangible effects of the difference, not the values themselves.* You generally cannot change the other person's values. You can, however, ask that they take certain actions.

*Practice active listening.* Don't glibly say, "I understand." Demonstrate your understanding by rephrasing what the other person has said. When this person feels that you understand her, the problem is half-solved in many cases. One of the most frequent causes of conflict is the feeling that the other party does not understand or appreciate your concerns.

*State what you want as a request, not as a demand.* Ask what the other person wants of you. If you cannot or will not comply with the other party's request, make a counterproposal. Try for win-win. Compromise only as a last resort.

*Keep in mind that the other person is not bad, mad, or crazy just because you have a difference.* If you judge people, it is hard to remain objective and to deal only with the issues.

*Try to work on one issue at a time when several exist.* Begin with those on which it is most likely that you will reach agreement.

*Don't rush the process.* Conflicts resolved in haste may come back to haunt you later.

*Once an agreement is reached, ask the other party if there is anything that might prevent their complying with the agreement.* Ask the same question of yourself. If there are potential obstacles, consider the contingencies that might arise. This is called doing an "ecology check" at the end of the negotiation. Failure to do so can result in a failed resolution of the conflict.

*Don't make promises you can't keep.* It is disastrous for a manager to promise something to an employee and then have his boss overrule him. If you need to check with your boss before making an agreement, say so and reconvene the meeting after you have seen your boss.

*Always give the other person a chance to save face.* Never belittle his position. Remember, all behavior makes sense from the perspective of the actor, if not from the perspective of the observer. If you fail to observe this rule, you may win the negotiation but make an enemy for life. And in the corporate world, this person may be your boss one day, or at least wait for an opportunity to stab you in the back to retaliate for your humiliating him.

### Exercises

1. Think of the conflicts you have been involved in recently. Of the five approaches to handling conflict, do you find yourself using one of them most of the time? If so, was that style always appropriate?

2. Do you ever avoid conflicts that should be confronted? Why do you think you do this? Is it because things might get emotional and you want to avoid such situations? Is it a fear of handling them badly?

3. Practice with friends some conflict situations that you want to learn to handle better. When you feel comfortable handling these in a skill-practice session, then try dealing with them "for real." You will find that practice makes it easier.

   You can buy an instrument for measuring your preferred conflict-handling style from Pfeiffer. Call 800-274-4434 for a catalog.

# CHAPTER 17

# Managing Team Capacity Issues

Project teams tend to be plagued by a common problem—they are always getting overloaded. When they complain of this to management, they are often met with disbelief. There are two primary reasons for this. One is management's notion that unless we challenge people they will slack off. Sometimes this is true. The second is that we often have no data to support our claim of being overloaded.

There is nothing wrong with challenging workers, of course, but when this is done by assigning targets that are virtually impossible to meet, the net result is to destroy incentive. In fact, in some organizations many targets are totally impossible to achieve in a normal forty-hour workweek, and so people are routinely forced to work fifty- and sixty-hour weeks in order to meet the challenges handed them by their managers.

I know that some managers consider such work schedules to be normal. After all, they will tell you, they themselves work long hours and they don't complain. The workers are just being wimpy. They also sometimes play a cost-justifying game by saying that the overtime hours are not only free when salaried people are involved but that even if you have to pay overtime wages, these are often cheaper than regular hours because the overhead costs have already been absorbed in a normal forty-hour week.

The problem with this argument is that it ignores hidden costs. These come in two major forms. One is turnover costs, which can easily be more than $100,000 to replace a professional person. The other is burnout costs. Studies show that in factory environments, after people have worked about three weeks of 50-hour weeks, their productivity is back down to the forty-hour level, and their error rate has increased. If you are paying

premium wages for that ten hours of overtime, you are losing money. Not only are you getting no increase in output; you are also now paying to correct the errors they have made. Similar statistics have been determined for knowledge workers. Surprisingly, they are only slightly different. The finding is that a knowledge worker who works fifty-five hours a week for several weeks actually accomplishes about forty-two hours of productive work. That is, thirteen hours are wasted.

This drop does not occur with overtime worked on an occasional basis. It occurs when it takes place over extended periods. And, because error rates go up, it can be attributed to fatigue. If the error rate stayed constant, you could conclude that pacing was behind it. That is, people are saying to themselves, "If I have to work a long stretch, I'm going to slow down, or else I won't be able to hold out that long."

# The Need for Keeping Skills Current

The second problem created by an organizational culture that expects fifty- to sixty-hour workweeks from its knowledge workers is obsolescence. We know that the half-life for engineers (of all kinds) is about two to five years unless they take training to keep their skills current. The term *half-life* comes from physics as applied to radioactive material, which decays over time. If you start with one gram of uranium, after a certain number of years only one-half gram will still be uranium. The remaining half gram will be something else. Applied to engineers, the statement means that half the technology they learned at a university will be obsolete in two to five years after they graduate. This is particularly obvious in computer technology, which is exploding at an accelerating rate.

What is significant is that whereas the skills of engineers are declining over time, the skills required to do their jobs are increasing. This is shown in Figure 17-1. As the curves show, when the engineer first graduates, there is a big gap in his favor. He has greater skills than are demanded by the job. Then, over time, he reaches a break-even point, where he has exactly the skills needed for the job. Past that point, he is losing ground, as the requirement is increasing at an exponentially accelerating rate, while he is just holding his own, more or less.

I'm afraid this phenomenon is used to justify getting rid of older engi-

**Figure 17-1.** Changing requirements for skills over time.

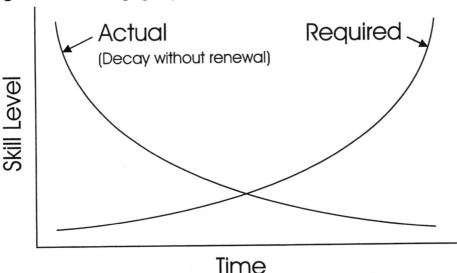

neers, and indeed engineers are definitely culpable when they do not maintain their skills. But how can they do so effectively when they spend so many hours working? It is very difficult.

Furthermore, organizations do not see the loss to themselves when professionals become obsolete. This would be more obvious if we did human resource accounting, an idea suggested by Peter Drucker in his book *Management: Tasks, Responsibilities, Practices* (1973). Considering that professional labor rates are in the range of $50 to $100 per hour, with overhead included, we are investing a minimum of $100,000 a year in each individual. Over a period of five years, that amounts to half a million dollars. If that money were invested in capital equipment, it would be depreciated, but an attempt would be made to protect the investment by maintaining the equipment. Yet we let our only truly renewable resource—a human being—figuratively rust away! It makes no economic sense, not to mention the cost to society in human suffering.

# Sharpening the Saw

Not only is the long-term decline in skills a problem, but long periods of overtime take their toll on day-to-day performance as well. In his book *The 7 Habits of Highly Effective People* (1990), Stephen Covey has said that one habit that makes people more effective is the habit of renewing themselves. He calls this "sharpening the saw," and tells a story to illustrate its importance.

Two woodcutters are cutting wood with saws. One of them works continually, hardly stopping even for a bio (biological) break. The other stops fairly frequently and disappears for a while. The worker who keeps his nose to the grindstone chides the other for his frequent breaks, but that woodcutter just ignores him. Even the onlookers think the man who takes so many breaks must be a skater.

At the end of the day, the foreman examines the piles of wood produced by the two men and, to his amazement, discovers that the man who took all those breaks has cut more wood than the other. So the foreman asks the woodcutter how he can explain his greater output, and he says it is very simple—he was taking breaks to sharpen his saw, so that when he was cutting wood, his efficiency was really high.

As Covey says, the analogy is easy to extend to people. If you work long hours and never stop to sharpen your "saw," you become dull and ineffective. Part of such saw sharpening should be aimed at maintaining one's technical skills, but the other should be for personal renewal only. We can think of people as having mind, body, and spirit, and all these must be maintained and kept in balance if the individual is to be fully effective. To maintain the spirit, a person might spend time listening to music, reading entertaining or thought-provoking material, or just visiting with good friends. Or he might go to church or meditate or read spiritual literature, depending on his inclination.

Maintaining body and mind are well understood; we need exercise and proper diet for the body, intellectual pursuits for the mind.

# Determining Team Capacity

If you ask a manufacturing manager to produce a certain amount of product in a given time frame, she can usually tell you fairly accurately whether it is possible in a normal forty-hour workweek or whether she will need to increase capacity by having people work longer hours. She can do this because manufacturing capacity is generally well defined.

This is seldom true in knowledge work areas, such as most project teams are involved in. It is true in construction projects where work processes are fairly well defined and where the time it takes to do certain jobs is backed up by good historical data. In fact, construction project managers have available data called *means tables* that tell them how much time to allow for pouring a certain amount of concrete or putting up structural steel. These tables are based on records kept for hundreds of construction projects.

Unfortunately, no such records exist for many project teams, or if they exist they are not useful. In the cases where statistical information exists, it is often for the project as a whole. We know how many working hours were required to complete the entire project, but not the amount of time needed for individual tasks within the project. So when we try to use the data to estimate another project duration, we have to extrapolate, since no two projects are ever exactly the same.

In fact, one way to get into real trouble is to base a project estimate on a project-to-project comparison. We often call such an estimate a ballpark estimate, and when these become targets, failure is often assumed.

In order to have usable information, we have to collect it on tasks that are repetitive. In terms of the Work Breakdown Structure (WBS), this means that the data must be collected at least down at the task, subtask, or work package level, this terminology being based on the model shown in Figure 17-2. When you are at the project level, it is not very often that two projects are exactly alike, so comparisons made on a project-to-project basis are inaccurate. Down at the lower levels of the WBS, however, we

**Figure 17-2.** WBS level names.

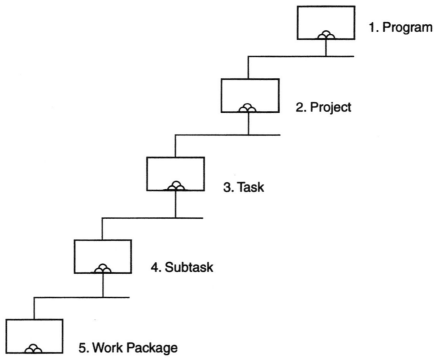

often have tasks that are repetitive, and data collected there can be used to estimate other similar tasks.

Another factor that affects the data is overtime. In a lot of companies, overtime for salaried people is not charged to a project in that no direct cost is involved. However, if you record forty working hours each week for your project, when you are really working sixty hours, then you have introduced a major error into the database and the next job will be estimated too low and people will wind up working overtime again to get the job done.

Finally, you have to forbid cross-charging. This is done when people are told to quit charging time to a project that is over budget and instead to charge their time to another project that is under budget. Doing so naturally makes both projects appear to come out on target, but one is artificially high and the other is artificially low. (Doing this on defense projects is actually illegal and will land you in jail.) The reason people do this is because the organization's culture prohibits going over or under budget. Such an outlook is unrealistic. There is variation in all processes, and to insist that budgets be met exactly is to insist that laws of nature be violated. You can reduce the variation in a process, but you can never eliminate it.

# The Effect of Multiple Projects on Capacity

Suppose I give you an assignment that you could complete in a single day if this assignment were the only thing you worked on. To keep the example simple, let's assume that this means you would work on it four hours in the morning and four hours in the afternoon. Naturally, you can't usually get uninterrupted blocks of time like this, but we will pretend that just this once it is possible.

Now let us inject a complication. Suppose I tell you that I just remembered—we have a company-wide meeting scheduled for all employees this afternoon. Attendance is mandatory, so you will only be able to work four hours this morning and you will have to come back tomorrow to finish up. Will you still finish the task in eight working hours?

The answer is no.

Why not? Because when you come in tomorrow, you will have to spend a few minutes getting reoriented to the job. We call this *setup time* in manufacturing. So an interruption causes the job to take longer.

Let's make it worse. I now tell you that you can work on the job for only two hours each day, spreading it out over four days. Will the job still take eight hours? No way. It will get even worse than it is for the two four-hour blocks because now you have setup time on four separate days. As you can see, reducing setup time increases productivity, a lesson manufacturing operations learned a long time ago.

The question is, what relevance does this have for projects?

The answer is that when people are assigned to multiple projects, they are constantly shifting back and forth among them, and this increases setup time, which reduces productivity. Interestingly, having a lot of projects in the hopper at once creates the illusion that a lot is going on, and it is; it just isn't very productive.

It is much more efficient and effective to prioritize your projects, get the high-priority ones done first, and then move to the next level. When you do this, they will still all get done in the same time frame (actually a shorter time frame), but they will be done a lot more efficiently. I know of one company that found its productivity actually doubled when it followed this approach, and I have a client who has achieved very good results the same way.

## Exercises

1. For the next two weeks, have each member of your team carry a log sheet and every hour record what he or she did during the previous hour. Then tally up the categories to find out where people are spending their time. You will probably find that none of them are spending more than 50 to 60 percent of their time doing project work. This is the figure that you must use in resource allocation if your schedule is to be meaningful. If this level is unacceptable, then you must find some way to increase team members' availability by removing the things that are robbing people of time.

2. Once you have collected data on how long various tasks take, ask entry-level members of your team to estimate the time needed for those tasks, then tell them the real figures. This is a good way to teach people how to make estimates without costing your organization anything for missed deadlines.

# Appendixes

# APPENDIX A

# Answers to
# Chapter Questions

**Chapter 2:**
1. **b**      3. **a**      5. **a**
2. **c**      4. **d**      6. **c**

**Chapter 9:**
1. You use participative style with the team, but you use directive or influence with the team member.
2. You should talk to his functional manager. If the problem cannot be resolved, you may have to remove him from your team.

**Chapter 10:**
1. This decision involves merit and acceptance. Both are important.
2. It is primarily acceptance, but you could argue that there is a small merit component.
3. They may try to infer her preference from her nonverbal behavior. Janis and Mann's procedure encourages all members to be critical evaluators in order to offset this tendency.
4. The false consensus effect is our tendency to assume that "silence means consent."
5. It is a failure to manage disagreement because everyone in the group assumed agreement and no one tried to find out if anyone disagreed. Had they done so, they would have avoided going to Abilene.

# APPENDIX B

# Resources for Project Managers

Following is a list of sources of information, books, and professional associations that may be helpful in managing projects. Not all are specifically aimed at project management, but you may find them helpful anyway.

**The Business Reader:** This is a mail-order bookstore specializing in business books. If it's on business, chances are they have it! P.O. Box 41268 • Brecksville, OH 44141 • Tel. (216) 838-8653 • FAX: (216) 838-8104.

**CRM Films:** A good source of films for training, including *Mining Group Gold, The Abilene Paradox*, and many others. 2215 Faraday Ave. • Carlsbad, CA 92008 • Tel. (800) 421-0833.

**The Lewis Institute, Inc.:** Founded by the author, the Institute provides training in project management, team building, and related courses. The core program is Project Management: Tools, Principles, Practices, which has been attended by about 13,000 managers worldwide. 302 Chestnut Mountain Dr. • Vinton, VA 24179 • Tel. (540) 890-1560 • FAX: (540) 890-7470 • James__Lewis__2@Compuserve.com.

**MindWare:** The store for the other 90 percent of your brain. A source of tools, books, and other materials for enhancing learning and creativity in organizations. It has a nice catalog listing its materials. 6142 Olson Mem. Hwy. • Golden Valley, MN. 55422 • Tel. (800) 999-0398 • FAX: (612) 595-8852.

**Morasco, Vincent:** A newspaper clipping service that operates on a pay-per-use basis. You pay only for the clippings you actually make use of. A good source of up-to-the-minute information. Vincent Morasco • 3 Cedar St. • Batavia, NY 14020 • Tel. (716) 343-2544.

**Pegasus Communications:** Publishers of *The Systems Thinker*, a monthly newsletter. It also has videos by Russell Ackoff and Peter Senge, among others. P.O. Box 943 • Oxford, OH 45056-0943 • Tel. (800) 636-3796 • FAX: (905) 764-7983.

**Pfeiffer & Company:** A source of training programs, training materials, instruments, and books on management. 350 Sansome St., 5th Floor • San Francisco, CA 94104 • Tel. (800) 274-4434 • FAX: (800) 569-0443.

**Pimsleur International:** The most effective way to learn a language on your own is with cassettes using a method developed by Dr. Paul Pimsleur. Learning is virtually painless. 30 Monument Square, Suite 135 • Concord, MA 01742 • Tel. (800) 222-5860 • FAX: (508) 371-2935.

**Project Management Institute:** The professional association for project managers, with over 10,000 members nationwide. It has local chapters in most major U.S. cities. 130 S. State Rd. • Upper Darby, PA 19082 • Tel. (610) 734-3330 • FAX: (610) 734-3266.

# References: Books and Articles for Further Reading

Ackoff, Russell. *The Art of Problem Solving*. New York: Wiley, 1978.

Adler, Paul, Avi Mandelbaum, Viên Nguyen, and Elizabeth Schwerer. "Getting the Most Out of Your Product Development Process," *Harvard Business Review*, March–April, 1996.

Albrecht, Karl. *The Northbound Train: Finding the Purpose, Setting the Direction, Shaping the Destiny of Your Organization*. New York: AMACOM, 1994.

Argyris, Chris. *Overcoming Organizational Defenses: Facilitating Organizational Learning*. Boston: Allyn and Bacon, 1990.

Barker, Joel. *Future Edge: Discovering the New Paradigms of Success*. New York: William Morrow and Company, 1992.

Bateson, Gregory. *Mind and Nature*. New York: Bantam Books, 1980.

Berne, Eric. *Games People Play*. New York: Grove Press, 1964.

Bienvenu, M. J., Sr. "An Interpersonal Communication Inventory," *The Journal of Communication* 21, no. 4 (1971), pp. 381–388.

Blake, Robert, and Jane Mouton. *The Managerial Grid*. Houston: Gulf Publishing, 1964.

*Boston Globe*. "Fast Track: Films Looking to Make Meetings More Productive." Staff Report, December 27, 1995.

Covey, Stephen. *The 7 Habits of Highly Effective People: Powerful Lessons in Personal Change*. New York: Fireside Books, 1990.

Cremo, Michael, and Richard Thompson. *The Hidden History of the Human Race*. Badger, Calif.: Govardhan Hill Publishing, 1994.

De Bono, Edward. *Serious Creativity*. New York: HarperCollins, 1992.

*Democrat and Chronicle* (Rochester, New York). "Work Study Points Out the Problem of 'Half-People.' " Staff Report, November 21, 1996.

Desloge, Rick. "At Your Service. To Satisfy Customers, Dierbergs, Boatmen's Start With Employees," *St. Louis Business Journal*, October 7–13, 1996.

Dimancescu, Dan. *The Seamless Enterprise*. New York: HarperBusiness, 1992.

Downs, Alan. *Corporate Executions: The Ugly Truth About Layoffs—How Corporate Greed Is Shattering Lives, Companies, and Communities*. New York: AMACOM, 1995.

Dressler, Catherine. "Organization, Planning Keep Meetings on Track," *Cleveland Plain Dealer*, February 11, 1996.

Drucker, Peter. *Management: Tasks, Responsibilities, Practices*. New York: Harper & Row, 1973, 1974.

Follett, Ken. *Pillars of the Earth*. New York: William Morrow and Company, 1989.

Fritz, Robert. *The Path of Least Resistance: Learning to Become the Creative Force in Your Own Life*. New York: Fawcett Columbine, 1989.

Haley, Jay. *Strategies of Psychotherapy*. New York: Grune & Stratton, 1986.

Hall, Doug. *Jump Start Your Brain: A Proven Method for Increasing Creativity Up to 500%!* New York: Warner Books, 1995.

Harris, Thomas. *I'm OK—You're OK*. New York: Avon Books, 1969.

Harvey, Jerry. *The Abilene Paradox and Other Meditations on Management*. Lexington, Mass.: Lexington Books, 1988.

Hendrick, Bill. "Disintegration of the Dream," *Atlanta Constitution*, August 18, 1996.

Hersey, Paul, and Kenneth Blanchard. *Management of Organizational Behavior*, 3d Ed. Englewood Cliffs, N.J.: Prentice Hall, 1972.

Janis, Irving, and Leon Mann. *Decision Making: A Psychological Analysis of Conflict, Choice, and Commitment*. New York: The Free Press, 1977.

Kelley, Robert, and Janet Caplan. "How Bell Labs Creates Star Performers," *Harvard Business Review*, July–August 1993, pp. 128–39.

Kirton, M. J. "Adaptors and Innovators: A Description and Measure," *Journal of Applied Psychology* 61, 1976.

Kormanski, Chuck, and Andrew Mozenter. "A New Model of Team Building: A Technology for Today and Tomorrow." In J. S. Pfeiffer, Editor, *The 1987 Annual: Developing Human Resources*. San Diego: University Associates, 1987.

Kouzes, James, and Barry Posner. *The Leadership Challenge: How to Get Extraordinary Things Done in Organizations*. San Francisco: Jossey-Bass, 1988.

Krackhardt, David, and Jeffrey Hanson. "Informal Networks: The Company Behind the Chart," *Harvard Business Review*, July–August 1993, pp. 104–111.

Kuhn, Thomas. *The Structure of Scientific Revolutions*, 2d Ed. Chicago: University of Chicago Press, 1970.

Lancaster, Hal. "Managing Your Career," *Wall Street Journal*, March 26, 1996.

Lerner, Michael. *The Politics of Meaning*. Reading, Mass.: Addison-Wesley, 1996.

Lewis, James. *Fundamentals of Project Management*. New York: AMACOM, 1993.

Lewis, James. *How to Build and Manage a Winning Project Team*. New York: AMACOM, 1993.

Lewis, James. *The Project Manager's Desk Reference*. Burr Ridge, Ill.: Irwin Professional Publishing, 1993.

Lewis, James. *Project Planning, Scheduling, and Control*, Rev. Ed. Burr Ridge, Ill.: Irwin Professional Publishing, 1995.

Lippincott, Sharon. *Meetings: Do's, Don'ts, and Donuts: The Complete Handbook for Successful Meetings*. Pittsburgh, Pa.: Lighthouse Point Press, 1994.

MacDonald, Gayle, "The Work and Family Juggling Act," *Toronto Globe and Mail*, January 2, 1996.

Malloy, John. *Dress for Success*. New York: Warner Books, 1993.

March, James, and Herbert Simon. *Organizations*. New York: Wiley, 1958.

Marshall, Stephanie. "Creating Sustainable Learning Communities for the Twenty-First Century." In *The Organization of the Future*, edited by Hesselbein, Goldsmith, and Beckhard. San Francisco: Jossey-Bass, 1997.

McClelland, David. *Power: The Inner Experience*. New York: Halsted Press, 1975.

Michalco, Michael. *Thinker Toys*. Berkeley, Calif.: Ten Speed Press, 1991.

Mintzberg, Henry. *Mintzberg on Management: Inside Our Strange World of Organizations*. New York: The Free Pres, 1989.

Molloy, John. *Dress for Success*. New York: Warner Books, 1993.

Mullins, Robert. "Dealing With the Demands of Family," *The Business Journal* (Milwaukee, Wis.), December 23, 1995.

Patterson, Marvin. *Accelerating Innovation: Improving the Process of Product Development*. New York: Van Nostrand, 1993.

Peters, Tom. *Liberation Management: Necessary Disorganization for the Nanosecond Nineties*. New York: Knopf, 1992.

Peters, Tom. *Thriving on Chaos: Handbook for a Management Revolution*. New York: Knopf, 1987.

Petzinger, Thomas, Jr., "The Front Lines," *Wall Street Journal*, January 3, 1997.

Ross, Sherwood. "Because of Layoffs, Suspicious Workers Look Out for No. 1," *Pittsburgh Post Gazette*, December 31, 1995.

Sabbagh, Karl. *Twenty-First-Century Jet: The Making and Marketing of the Boeing 777*. New York: Scribner, 1996.

Schutz, Will. *The Interpersonal Underworld*. Palo Alto, Calif.: Science and Behavior Books, 1966.

Schwarz, Roger. *The Skilled Facilitator: Practical Wisdom for Developing Effective Groups*. San Francisco: Jossey-Bass, 1994.

Senge, Peter. *The Fifth Discipline*. New York: Doubleday, 1990.

Stacey, Ralph. *Managing the Unknowable: Strategic Boundaries Between Order and Chaos in Organizations*. San Francisco: Jossey-Bass, 1992.

Stevenson, H. W. "Learning from Asian Schools," *Scientific American*, December 1992.

Stevenson, H. W., and J. W. Stigler. *The Learning Gap: Why Our Schools Are Failing and What We Can Learn from Japanese and Chinese Education*. New York: Summit, 1992.

Tuckman, Bruce W. *Development Sequence in Small Groups*, Psychological Bulletin, 1965.

Uris, Alan. *The Executive Deskbook*, 3d Ed. New York: Van Nostrand, 1988.

Vincent, James L. "Today's Work Force Needs New Leaders," *Boston Globe*, September 17, 1996.

Von Oech, Roger. *A Kick in the Seat of the Pants*. New York: Perennial Library, 1986.

Walton, Mary. *The Deming Management Method*. New York: Dodd, Mead & Company, 1986.

Weisbord, Marvin. *Productive Workplaces: Organizing and Managing for Dignity, Meaning, and Community*. San Francisco: Jossey-Bass, 1987.

Wheatley, Margaret. *Leadership and the New Science: Learning About Organization from an Orderly Universe*. San Francisco: Berrett-Koehler, 1994.

# Index

# Index

# About the Author

James P. Lewis is the founder of The Lewis Institute, Inc., an association of professionals providing project management training and behavioral consulting to organizations throughout the United States, Canada, Mexico, England, and the Far East. This includes training in team building, engineering management, and problem solving given to several Fortune 100 and 500 companies in the United States. Jim has also conducted team training workshops for organizations in Bintulu, Sarawak, and Surabaya, Indonesia.

An outstanding workshop leader, he has trained more than 16,000 managers and supervisors since 1981, drawing on his many years of first-hand experience as a manager with ITT Telecommunications and Aerotron, Inc., where he held positions including Product Engineering Manager, Chief Engineer, and Project Manager. He also served as Quality Manager for ITT Telecom during the last two years of his industrial career. During his fifteen years as an electrical engineer, Jim designed and developed a variety of communications equipment for application in land, sea, and mobile environments. He holds a joint patent on a programmable memory for a transceiver.

He has published numerous articles on managing as well as four books on project management: *How to Build and Manage a Winning Project Team* and *Fundamentals of Project Management*, both published by AMACOM Books; and *Project Planning, Scheduling, and Control* (rev. ed.) and *The Project Manager's Desk Reference*, published by Irwin Professional Publishing of McGraw-Hill. He holds a B.S. in Electrical Engineering and both M.S. and Ph.D. degrees in Psychology, all from North Carolina State University.

Jim is married to the former Lea Ann McDowell, and they live in Vinton, Virginia, in the Blue Ridge Mountains. Although they have no children of their own, they have three exchange student "daughters," Yukiko Bono of Japan, Katarina Sigerud of Sweden, and Susi Mraz of Austria.

You can contact Jim at the Lewis Institute, Inc. See the Resources for Project Managers section (Appendix B) for phone numbers and e-mail address.